A Sunset Book

PLANNING AND LANDSCAPING Hillside Homes

By the editorial staffs of
Sunset Books and Sunset Magazine

LANE BOOKS • MENLO PARK, CALIF.

Acknowledgments

Many individuals, business firms, and public and private agencies helped in the preparation of this book. The editors would like to specially thank Robert Iacopi for securing and verifying a vast amount of information on legal and semi-legal aspects of hillside home buying; California Redwood Association, West Coast Lumbermen's Association, Western Pine Association, American Plywood Association, Bethlehem Steel Company, Southern California Edison, Pacific Gas & Electric, and Puget Sound Power and Light for information on building materials and techniques; and the Black Mountain Soil Conservation District and the Soil Conservation Service of the United States Department of Agriculture, which are jointly pioneering in the area of converting open land to urban use on a planned basis.

Ninth Printing March 1972

 LIBRARY OF CONGRESS CATALOG CARD NUMBER 65-16751. TITLE NUMBER 540. LITHOGRAPHED IN THE UNITED STATES OF AMERICA.

Contents

Sinagua Indian dwelling, Arizona.

Taormina, Sicily; founded 397 B.C.

Introduction: Going the extra mile is what

Many of the first men lived on hillsides, in caves, for reasons they seldom or never stopped to think out.

Hillside home sites have been popular through all the tumultuous ages of man since the stone ages. Increasingly the desire to live high on a slope has become a reasoned one. In our present state of civilization the old business of having a good angle on the tiger when he charges hardly matters at all. In fact, the simple problems of daily life are a bit tougher on the hill than they are down on the flat.

It is the going of the extra mile that makes hillside living attractive, or even an adventure.

The hill dweller can usually make good use of all the ideas he can gather. He knows that designing a hillside house, building it into its site, and living in it afterwards without inconvenience often calls for the most careful consideration of a number of absorbing problems.

When planning the house, a host of questions press for answer: Should the house face into the view or take it in sideways? should the terrace be on the view side or the blind side of the house? where should the family car be stored? on a hillside site, what rooms should be planned for street level? how plan for outdoor living on a site that would delight a mountain goat? how is a deck supported? what plants thrive on a slope? and what can be done to prevent or stop erosion?

Often, the advantages peculiar to living on a hill exact their price. With the view may come a glare problem. The gentle uphill breezes sometimes gang together and scourge the house and garden. Careful interior planning is needed to prevent development of tiring stair traffic. The soaring freedom of the deck often calls for a stabilizing element to make it seem safe and secure.

These are some of the problems that

Motrico, Spain; medieval town.

Edinburgh, Scotland; old city dates from 1100s.

makes hillside living an adventure

the owners and skilled designers of the homes shown in this book had to face and solve.

If you are in the planning stage of developing a hillside house, perhaps you can gain some useful ideas from studying these homes. If you are planning to remodel an existing hill-house, perhaps you can find an idea for adding a deck, for making cannier use of interior space, or for gaining more living space in your sloping garden.

The means exist in greater variety than they ever have before. The pictures on these two pages show examples of hillside architecture from several places and periods. Without exception, the technique was to make a masonry box, with the first floor level established by the highest point of the grade level. Also, they show a general predilection toward outcroppings of rock, which could be counted upon to be stable if not richly promising as garden sites.

On the next page, and thereafter, you see some examples of the genius of contemporary American manufacturers, architects, landscape architects, and builders. They have devised practical methods for hanging spacious platforms in mid-air over steep slopes of unstable clay soils—and in the process have worked out ways to make them seem snug and friendly structures.

Among the homes shown in these pages, the standard wood-framed structure predominates. But there are exciting variations in masonry, post-and-beam construction with either dimensioned timbers or peeled poles, and, last but not least, steel.

Many architects and homeowners resisted steel through the 1950's because it seemed cold and forbidding in residential buildings. The resistance has faded, and continues to fade steadily as imaginative examples spring up on hillsides in cities and towns all over the

Sausalito, California; the town is venerable, but none of these buildings predates the mid-1950's.

More about hillside homeowning...

nation. Steel frames can use any kind of sheet material or masonry in non-structural walls—a steel-framed adobe house can be less expensive than one made conventionally with adobe because it doesn't need the same kind of stout reinforcement.

Techniques with wood have advanced apace, however, and glue-laminated beams offer the same kind of reach capacity within the main frame of a building that steel does. Box beams using plywood "skin" are another development in wood, holding promise of dramatic platforms and cantilevers.

Along with all of this progress, landscape architects have responded to the challenges of engineering gardens onto unlikely looking slopes. Their experiments with plant materials and planting techniques have contributed not only to the beauty of gardens but to the general safety of many hillside building sites.

In these pages are depicted some dramatic results of hillside architecture and landscaping. The word "results" needs some stressing. The book is not intended as a "how-to" manual, but rather as a collection of ideas. In fact, there are times when the text may sound somewhat like a waspish schoolmaster warning students of the dire perils that follow any failure to observe the Golden Rule. There are repeated warnings to inquire at official agencies, or to enlist the help of professionals. There are repeated cautions against doing it yourself.

The warnings are there because any number of instructive examples were set during the preparation of the book, when heavy winter rains caused several gardens to go visiting at the neighbors in communities only a few miles away from the Sunset offices, and when the courts found the County of Los Angeles responsible for the collapse of several hillside homes because it graded a road in a way that upset natural drainage patterns in the lots below.

Hillside homesites offer great advantages to their owners—ones that cannot be matched by sites in the lowlands—but the advantages turn to grief if the site is not developed with full knowledge that something as minor as clearing off some unsightly weeds can, in time, lead to radical changes in the drainage patterns of the soil. It is the professional who knows how to reap benefit from change.

Small Homes

The homes shown in this chapter range in size from 800 to 1200 square feet in floor area. Most of them were designed specifically for couples or for single persons living alone.

No particular mode of construction underlies the collection, as is the case in the three succeeding chapters describing homes for hillsides. The houses resemble each other in two respects: They are fairly easy to maintain (indoors and out), and their construction costs were relatively little.

Both qualities have wide appeal to shrinking families and to retired persons. Indeed, one description or the other applies to the owners of each of the five homes shown in the main section of the chapter, and to all but one of the owners of homes shown only by floor plan on page 18.

In many cases small buildings will fit handily on sites that would be impractical for a larger structure, or for a family with children. Such lots may be less costly than a typical lot in a flat subdivision. So long as the inconveniences of longer shopping trips and more stairs do not outweigh the savings, the pleasures of hillside homeowning are extra dividends.

Stories of houses shown on this page are to be found: top photo, page 14; next photo, page 10; third photo, page 16; and bottom photo, page 8.

View of house *from the street. Steps at right quickly top the steep bank, then 3-foot square concrete pads provide a gentler ascent to the house. Six-foot overhang on roof is a shield against setting sun. Entry is at rear.*

Ideas aplenty for a small hillside home

ARCHITECT: HENRY HILL

For the person who is thinking of building a small residence or a weekend retreat, here is a provocative example.

The house sits far back on a fairly steep lot with a sweeping view of San Francisco Bay. Its floor area is about 620 square feet, divided into living room, dining alcove, kitchen, bedroom, and bath. The extensive use of glass and the high ceiling make the house seem more spacious than it really is. The owner can see out of every room; even the bathroom has a large glass window opening on a garden of its own. (For closer looks at such gardens, see p. 79.)

By the entry is a protected patio. The property's landscaping has been kept simple, designed for low maintenance. Generous use is made of ground covers and evergreen plants that do not need special watering or pruning.

Here is how the house evolved: The property owner wanted a house designed by an architect, and a garden designed by a landscape architect. She asked architect Hill whether this were possible at a cost of not more than $11,000 (in 1955). The architect accepted the challenge. The house shown in these photographs cost less than $11,000, including lot, architect's fees, and landscape architect's fees. Eckbo, Dean & Williams designed the garden.

There was no need for a car shelter. The owner has no car, and uses Berkeley public transportation which passes only half a block from the door.

To cut costs the house was designed in square and rectangular forms. The bedroom and bath were placed at a higher level than the living room and kitchen to save on excavation (the terrace is the only other excavated area). The owner did all the planting and some of the garden construction work herself.

Compact kitchen *has wall oven, washing machine, refrigerator recessed in partition. Work stool tucks under counter.*

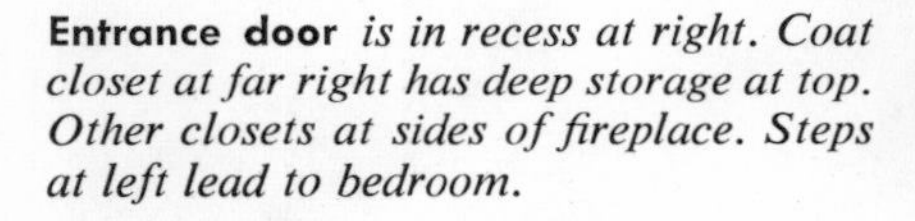

Entrance door *is in recess at right. Coat closet at far right has deep storage at top. Other closets at sides of fireplace. Steps at left lead to bedroom.*

Site plan *shows plant materials, chosen for easy maintenance.*

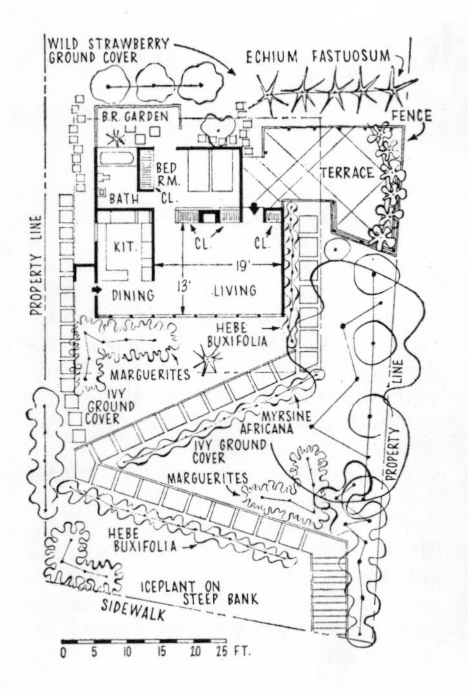

Side of house *is glass, so there is plenty of light, and a feeling of space. Bookcase is built in, but dining tables can be moved to living room if needed.*

Street entrance *to deck is at far right. Deck drains to gravel fill below, and is sheltered by extended walls of house and by lush growth of shrubs. The latter hide the house from the street, so there are no draperies on living room windows.*

An open deck, open plan

ARCHITECT: PAUL HAYDEN KIRK

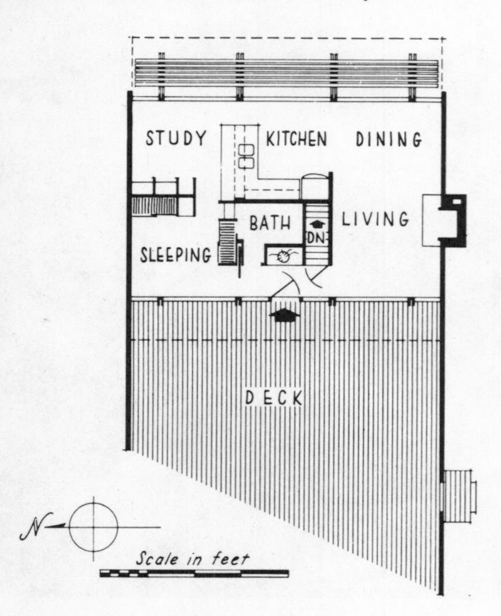

Floor plan *shows core design clearly. Heavy arrow indicates the entry.*

This small Northwest house is notable for three things: It has an outdoor room which almost doubles the usable floor space of the house five months out of the year. It is a fine example of an economical open plan, created around a central core. And it proves that elegance can be achieved without using expensive materials.

The windowless side walls of the house are extended to enclose the sun trap deck on two sides; there is complete privacy from neighboring lots. The three walls and a leafy screen on the fourth side produce the illusion that the deck is a room. The illusion is heightened further by standing on the deck and looking through the living room to the view beyond.

The central core of the house contains a bathroom, storage space, and a stairway to the basement room. Skylights and an electric fan provide sufficient light and ventilation for the bathroom. All other rooms look out on the enclosed deck or to the view in the distance. The walls, ceiling, and beams of the interior are of Douglas fir, stained and burned with ferrous chloride.

A catwalk extending from the east wall makes window washing possible (see p. 70 for other ideas).

The basement room contains the furnace and laundry and provides valuable storage space. Walls could enclose the entire space below the house to make additional bedrooms should the need arise.

Simple *dramatic entrance leads to deck through opening in windowless side wall.*

Living room *(top) walls, ceiling and beams are of Douglas fir, stained and burned with ferrous chloride. Below, living room viewed from entry.*

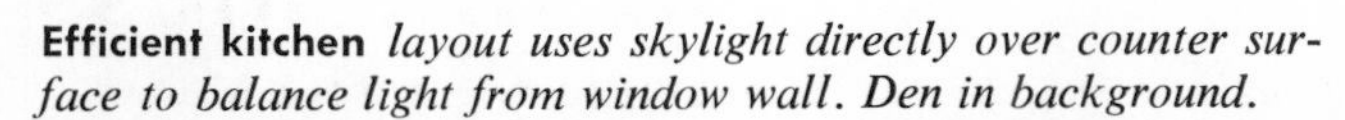

Efficient kitchen *layout uses skylight directly over counter surface to balance light from window wall. Den in background.*

Side view *shows how house is planned to minimize cutting into Seattle hillside. Catwalk aids window-washing on view side.*

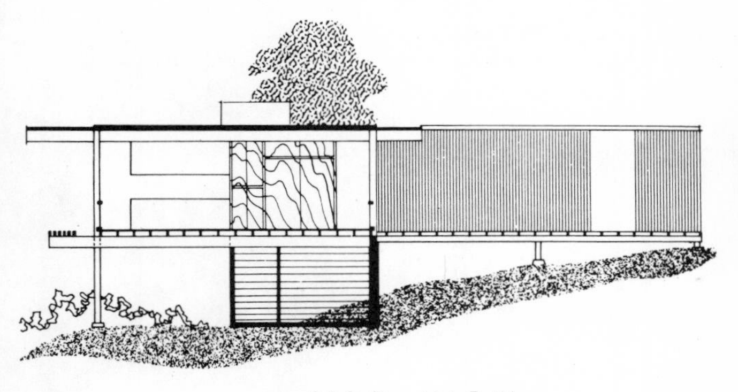

Deck *off the living room. Steps turn and lead down to basement shop. The small opening in the deck is for small oak.*

No smallness

ARCHITECT: MORTON & MILLER

Sketch *of house shows how roof extends to include carport and entry, and also how the roof helps to protect some of the deck areas from hot sun.*

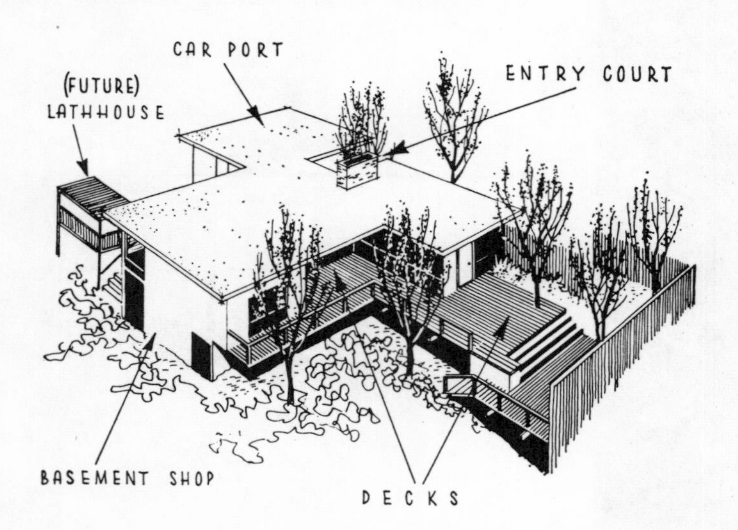

On a less precipitous site than the house shown on the pages preceding, this design still attempts to achieve similar effects of openness and spaciousness through the use of decks around a core plan.

The owners faced the usual choices open to young families: 1) Build more house than they actually need or want at the moment, or 2) build the core of a larger house with the idea of adding on when the need arises later.

The owners took a third course. They built a good house designed only to meet their existing needs. They considered the house complete when the hammers stopped for the first time. When they have outgrown the house, they plan to rent it or to sell it to new owners who seek a small home.

View *into trees from dining room. Living room wall at left.*

From dining room, *back wall of the fireplace is visible at left.*

Exposed beams, *cork floor enhance informality of living room.*

in this house

The photographs show how the house seems large because of its open walls, which allow the borrowing of space from outdoors. The enclosed all-weather space is only 836 square feet (plus an additional 240 square feet in a basement shop). The roof, including extensive overhangs, gives some protection over 1,600 square feet of usable space (most of the additional amounts above decks which have a total surface of 700 square feet). House walls extend to enclose an entry court, to shelter the living room deck, and to hide a service yard.

Native trees, though not impressive in size, were saved to protect the house with a light, high screen of twigs and branches. They cast an ever-changing pattern of light and shadow on the deck and indoors in this Eugene, Ore., home.

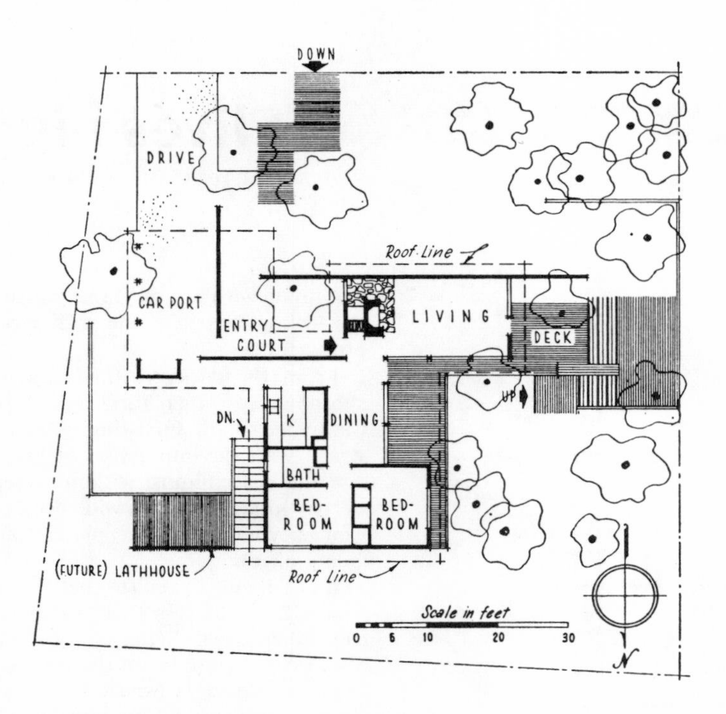

From below *you see the cantilevered deck and sweep of roof above. Skylight lets light through to back of deck and inside of the house. Glass cover provides protection for furniture on the deck. Lattice on back of carport shades hanging fuchsias.*

It lives bigger than it looks

ARCHITECT: MARQUIS & STOLLER

Plan *shows good arrangement of deck, living areas. Service yard is convenient.*

N
CAR PORT
0 5 10 FEET
STORAGE
DECK
DINING
SERVICE YARD
KITCHEN
PREVAILING WINDS
LIVING
BATH
ENTRY
BEDROOM
GUEST AND STUDY

Beginning with its entry, this house gives the feeling that it is one with generous proportions.

From the deck, visitors step into a short hallway, then turn right to enter the living room. First-time guests seem struck with the impression of luxurious size and space almost without exception as they look across the wide deck to the view beyond (see the photo on the facing page).

It is difficult to realize that the house is small. It has less than 1,400 square feet of enclosed living space. But the walls do not close in on the rooms. The feeling of space is especially surprising since it is achieved without using an open plan. The living room, dining room, and deck are open to one another, but the kitchen is entirely closed off.

Here are some of the techniques the designers used to achieve the feeling of space:

- Raised the ceiling height a little higher than usual—the plate height is nine feet—to give each room more volume and make the ceiling seem lighter.
- Kept wall and ceiling surfaces plain and uncluttered.
- Used generous decks to extend the floor of the house outdoors on two sides.
- Gave the entire southeast corner of the living area a wall of glass.

Living area *and deck look out over hills near Santa Rosa, Calif. Floor, ceiling designed to tie indoors, outdoors together, with minimum separation by window wall. Hinged vents at left allow ventilation. Dining room around corner at right.*

Entry deck *is more than 6 feet wide, 10 feet long. Service yard is behind grapestake fence at right of picture.*

In kitchen, *range top is set in combination work and breakfast table. Washer-dryer in separate room (behind camera).*

Spaciousness *of one-room house is shown in this photograph from the living area looking back to kitchen (behind the screened cabinets), and up to the bedroom balcony. The dining area is to the left, and the entry is beyond it.*

A small house is snug on a windy hill

ARCHITECT: ROBERT J. PETERSON

In a great many of the hill suburbs homeowners need protection from strong winds and from summer sun to enjoy living outdoors. This design not only solves these problems but also makes a small house seem spacious.

Architect Peterson provided several built-in climate controls (the wind is from the north in Yakima, Wash.). An extension of the north wall protects the view deck from wind. The south glass areas are shaded—in the living area by the low roof overhang, in the dining room area by the sun shade over a garden court (it is made of plastic panels set in an egg-crate-type framework), and in the bedroom by a louver grille outside the window. On the west, the glass is under roof. The garden court (the only planted area on a rambling site) is walled for privacy and wind shelter.

With its open plan inside—horizontally and vertically—the house is much more varied and spacious than you might expect possible in a one-room structure, and it is much cooler in summer, too.

On a *grass-covered hillside, only landscaping is in a court; tree above wall of house marks its location.*

Living room *overlooks hill-rimmed city visible beyond edge of deck. Wind baffle (left) extends roof line.*

From kitchen *counter you see dining area, spiral stairs to balcony. Entry is just out of picture to right.*

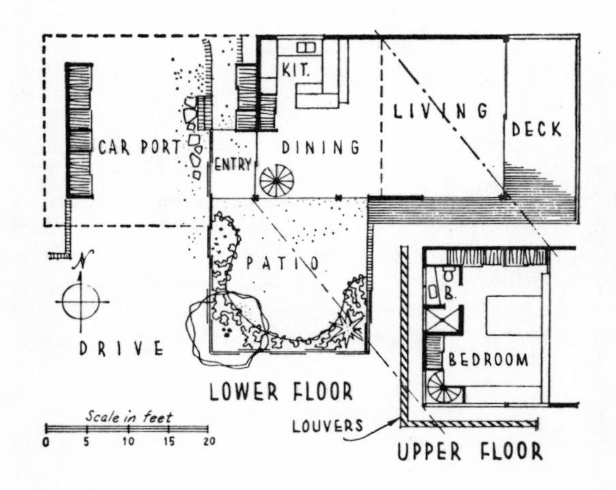

Bedroom *is open to living room below, but cabinet parapet screens it from view. Louvers baffle noonday sun.*

More small home plans

Spacious deck *with wind baffle is the key to livability in this small house. House has only 830 sq. ft. of floor. The deck adds another 300 square feet. It is on the downhill side of the house, directly off a living room with a raised-hearth fireplace. Wide, sliding glass doors connect the two, and make the living room seem spacious even in bad weather. The owner architect is Jon Konigshofer.*

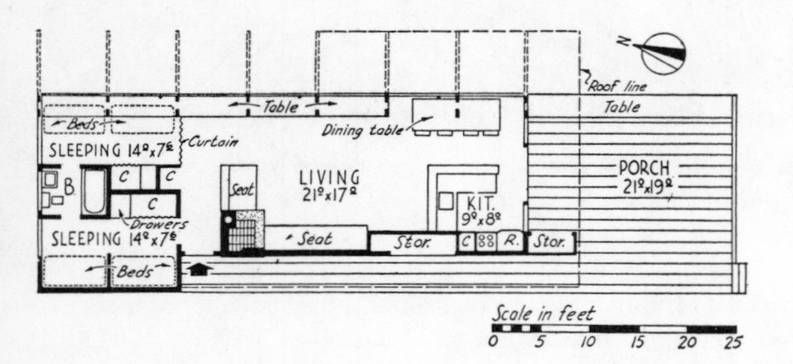

A weekend house *or a small house for year-around living, this platform structure commands a sweeping view across steeply tumbling hills. The side shown at the bottom of the floor plan is at grade level; the other side is several feet above grade. The downhill side has a window wall; clerestory windows on the upslope wall balance the light. The architect was Fred Langhorst.*

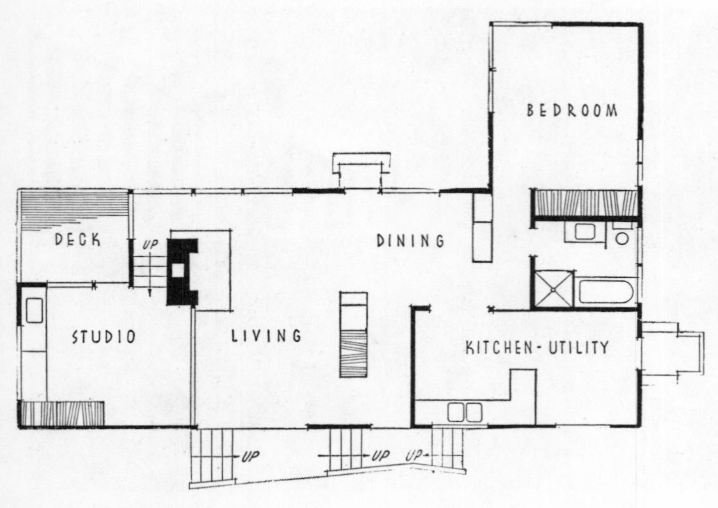

A single, *well-chosen extravagance added a feeling of luxury far out of proportion to the added cost to this house. The luxury was a studio set three steps up from the main floor level of the house. It is at the downhill side of the building, above the garage. A window looks into the living room, and another looks out over the deck, adding to the apparent size. The architect was Norris Gaddis.*

Two-story Homes

Two-story homes, or even taller ones, take up the next 17 pages of this book. The examples represent solutions by outstanding architects to difficult sites.

Typically, the homes are on lots where outdoor living space could be achieved only by stacking the house on a small base . . . or on still more difficult sites where outdoor living space could be achieved only by means of decks or roof gardens.

Stories of houses shown on this page are to be found: top photo, page 22; next photo, page 34; third photo, page 27; and bottom photo, page 32.

Responses evoked by this challenge range over a wide number of building techniques, materials, and divisions of space.

Two-story homes pose the greatest number of potential sources of annoyance to the owners if some point goes awry in the design. Which rooms on which level? Where to put access points to the garden? How to orient the structure to get the best from the view without exposing every room to an unfavorable amount of sunshine? Too little may be as vexing as too much.

In addition to comparing floor plans in this section to see how they might meet their own needs, shoppers for two-story homes might also wish to look at the sections on stairs (pp 66-69) and labor savers (p 70).

To take *advantage of slope, carport is at lowest level. Entry walk is on far side of stone wall. Patio, at intermediate level, is visible just above car roof. At top level, living room is at right while dining room and kitchen are at left. The deck is used for summer dining, in an area warm enough to require sunshade over west windows.*

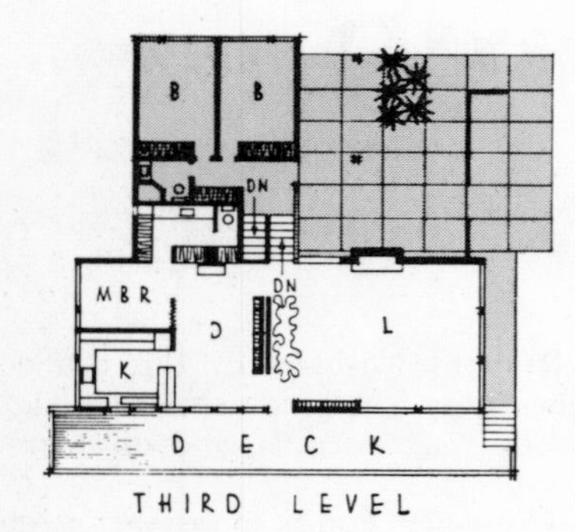

SECOND LEVEL

0 5 10 15 FEET

N

WORKROOM

CARPORT

FIRST LEVEL

The owners built high to capture a fine view

ARCHITECT: PAUL HAYDEN KIRK

This ranch house also happens to contain some good ideas for cabin planning. It was originally intended mainly for summer use, with only occasional winter visits. So the architect grouped a "living unit"—dining room (which serves as a general assembly hall), kitchen, master bedroom, and bath—where it could be heated separately from the rest of the house. The master bedroom, a sitting room by day, opens to the dining room by means of a folding door, for more living area. To capitalize on a sweeping view, this unit is at the top level of the house.

A bedroom for the owner's teen-age son and a guest bedroom are placed lower, level with a sheltered patio. These rooms and the living room are heated by electric space heaters when necessary. At the lowest level are the carport and a large summer workroom.

Bedroom wing *is to right of sheltered patio. Entry and stairs are in shadow under trellis to right of chimney.*

Living room, *looking toward west windows. Fireplace, of stones gathered on site (as is wall beneath house), has brown-black hue to complement the warm color of redwood walls, and walnut parquet floors.*

Kitchen *is compact, has no through traffic. Windows face due east, and those to left look north across the deck. This view is across the serving counter, from the dining room.*

Dining room. *Desk-and-storage cabinet has fixed plastic panels above. Glass panes above sliding panel track. Sliding panels can shut off dining room, kitchen, bedroom for separate heating.*

From below, *visitors can see the deck jutting out around three sides of the large-windowed living room. The view is out over forests surrounding Milwaukie, Ore. The panorama has a pleasantly contrasting garden that is screened from the street on the upslope side of the house. The exterior of the house is resawn cedar siding.*

Simply built...in a local tradition

ARCHITECT: JOHN STORRS

A descendant of a long and honest design tradition stemming from the barns and ranch houses of eastern Oregon, this house does much more than fit gracefully into its site and climate. It provides its owner with generous, usable space for varied activity, and proves you can still build a "carpenter's house" at relatively low cost.

Designed for a single woman, it has 1,600 square feet of living space, plus a garage and a basement on the steep downslope. Simple detailing and natural finishing kept the cost down and give the house a warm, informal air.

The division of the living area creates a pleasant contrast of sheltering low ceilings in the dining room, a sitting alcove by the fireplace, and a balcony studio with the two-story spaciousness of the living room itself, open through glass to surrounding trees.

The views also contrast pleasantly, an intimate courtyard opposes a larger outlook over forest. The forest view expands upon itself in winter when deciduous trees offer bare branches to the sky. The balcony around the living room gives that room a further feeling of continuity with the outdoors, and provides level space for outdoor living above the steep slope when the courtyard is too sunny.

Entry *is trim and inviting. Stripped sapling posts carry out the native feel of the structure. The dining room looks out into the pleasant small garden (left of photo).*

Cool green *forest view changes in winter to vista of Mount Hood. Rear wall of fireplace (right) sets off space for sitting area around hearth, under low ceiling.*

Floor plan *places kitchen between street, living areas. Bedrooms also separate from public area of house.*

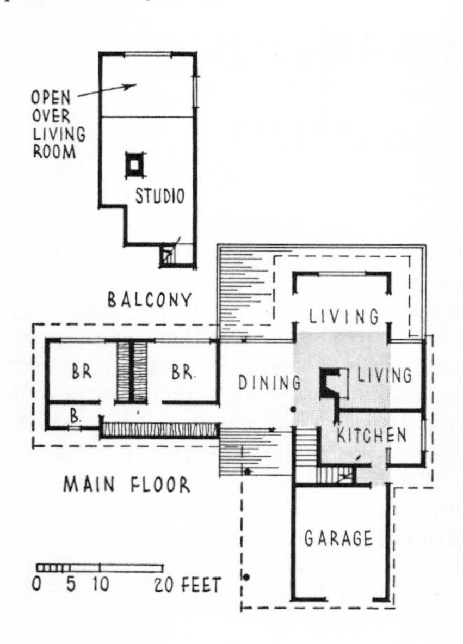

Snug studio *in low-headroom balcony looks across two-story living room to forest. Studio lit by clerestory windows.*

Kitchen, *with breakfast table in foreground. Light diffusing panels overhead provide glare-free work light for cook.*

Separation *between the upper (living) terrace and the lower (recreation) terrace makes it possible to use them both without undue conflict. The deck serves as an extension for the living area. Concrete terrace for dining and entertaining is on extreme left. Railing along deck and upper lawn is pipe set in wood posts. There are steps to the lower level at end of lawn.*

Indoor-outdoor living on two levels

ARCHITECT: ROBERT BILLSBROUGH PRICE

This is not a house with a garden around it. The house and garden were designed and developed together as an environment. This kind of planning makes a house more than a house, and a garden more than a garden. It can be practiced with any lot, with a house of any size or architectural type.

The garden starts at the lot lines and takes advantage of every inch of ground on a sloping site on the shore of American Lake, on the outskirts of Tacoma. The garden surrounds the house in a way that gives each room a view of its own, out to the tree-fringed horizon or into an intimate corner. These varied outlooks give the house a refreshing change of pace and increase the feeling of close relationship between house and garden.

The owners wanted a two-story house, which required grading the lot to help keep the silhouette of the house low and in keeping with the gentle slopes around it. The garden designed by Lawrence Halprin was worked out along with the house, before any grading was done.

With two adults and three children in the family, the house had to be large, yet the owners wanted the intimate qualities of a small home. The division between levels of both building and garden met this demand. The upper level is the living area, and it is meant for adult use (or for quiet use by the youngsters). The lower level is given over entirely to recreational pursuits.

Exterior siding and inside wood walls are rough-sawn cedar. Ceilings and soffits (area under roof overhang) are plastic impregnated plywood. The plastic keeps the plywood grain from raising.

Fireplace wall *in living room includes bookshelves, phonograph (above wood bin), television (behind screen).*

Dining area *is separated from kitchen by wall of louvers. Sliding door by drapery allows easy access to kitchen.*

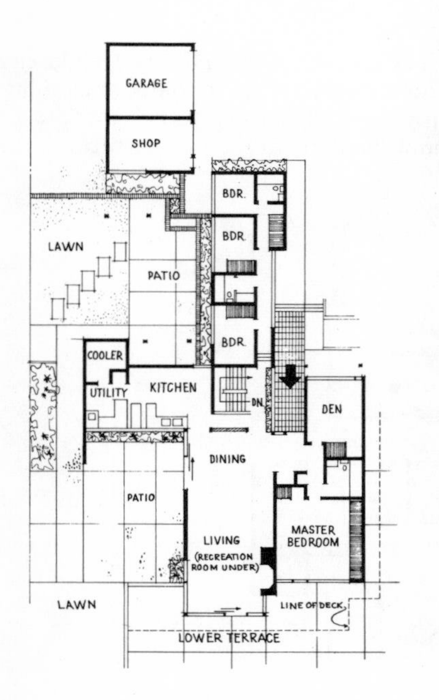

Glass wall *at end of living room looks over lake to the trees on far shore. In good weather Mount Rainier looms on the horizon. Sliding doors open to the terrace (right) and to the deck. Recreation room is directly below.*

Kitchen, *utility, and small dining space are all in this separate wing (see floor plan at left), which helps to create a private family patio just outside the bedroom area. The kitchen windows look out on main patio.*

Living room. *Raised hearth for seating in lower left corner of photo is placed to permit long view out over city of Spokane. Interior wall (right) compares closely in appearance to exterior walls of house. Deck is for window washing.*

Living on the upper level... sleeping below

ARCHITECT: WALKER, MCGOUGH AND TROGDON

The two critical requirements for this house were that it fit a family of two adults and four young children, and that it take advantage of its hillside view north across the city spreading out below.

The living area—living room and family room-kitchen—is on the upper level where large windows open it up to the view. The entrance is midway between the floors. The lower floor is the sleeping floor, with bedrooms facing the view. Grouped on the side against the hill are baths and heater, storage, and utility rooms.

Kitchen work, family dining, and informal living are all in one large room. Beyond this room's fireplace wall and isolated from the rest of the house is the more formal living room with its own secluded, roofed terrace. There is no formal dining room. The owners set up a buffet at one end of the living room for dinner parties. They felt isolation from the noisy activities of the children was worth more than closeness to the kitchen.

A feature of the plan is a children's corner with storage for outdoor clothing, toys, and other gear next to the kitchen and the door to the play terrace.

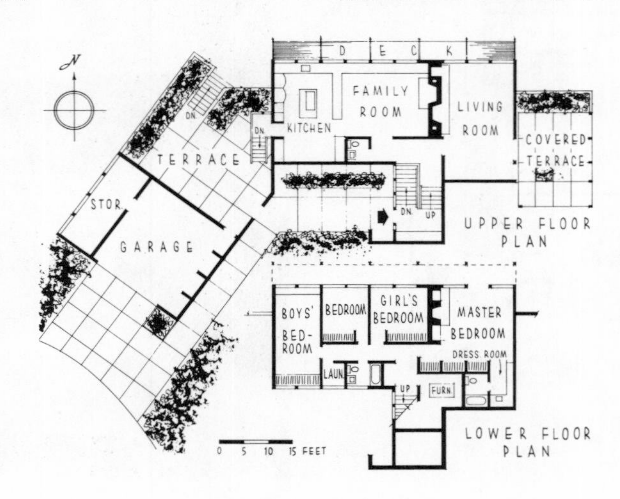

Family room *is tied to kitchen closely, but is screened by a high counter. Big dining table hidden by the counter.*

From downhill *the large windows of the living area are above the deck; bedroom windows below. Terrace at left.*

Master bedroom *is fitted out as study and sitting room. Desk and bookshelves are out of photo to left.*

Large bedroom *for two boys is 10 by 21 feet. Built-in desk-and-drawers at one end; huge closets cover other end.*

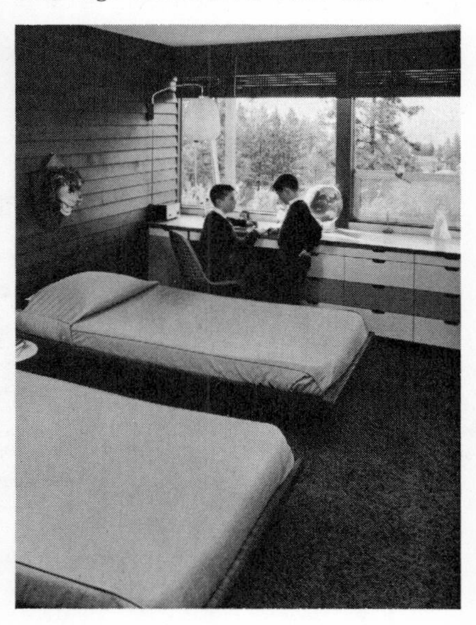

House *sits below level of the street, its low forms emphasizing horizontal lines. Hole in roof at right locates the garden court.*

Living and dining around a garden court

ARCHITECT: FISK AND HODGKINSON

A garden court and high, clerestory-lit ceilings in the living area make this house seem spacious despite its moderate size. Architects and landscape architect worked together to preserve and integrate into the design the fine trees on the steeply pitched site. The view out through the trees to the rear was an important factor in the living area arrangement.

Turned away from the street that runs above it, the house sits low and snug. From the inside, it literally opens out to a garden, a deck, and a long view.

The house is carefully zoned to fit the family's needs.

The children's rooms fill one wing of the cross-shaped plan. The master bedroom is close by, but in a separate wing. The ceiling in the children's wing is standard height. The master bedroom shares the high, pecky cedar ceiling of the living area.

The contrast in distribution of rooms between the floors in this case and in the example on the preceding pages could scarcely be stronger. It demonstrates how much slope and view can do to alter the living conditions of essentially similar families.

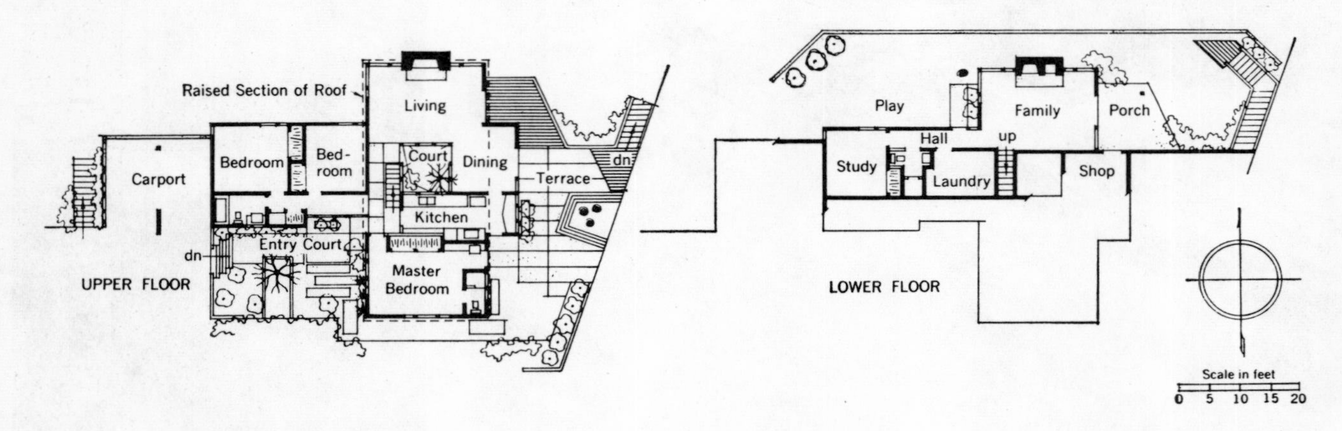

Beyond *the glass walls of the living room is a fine view of native trees.*

Garden court *is focal point of the house, and a source of light for all living areas. Clerestory windows add to the high daylight above bedroom wing.*

Terrace *is well-shaded by old oak. It adjoins the dining room (large windows) and can be seen from the kitchen (windows at left).*

Breakfast *counter at end of narrow kitchen faces terrace alongside house.*

Two-way *slope (left to right, rear to front) called for formal entry stairway. Private deck off parlor, behind wall above carport. Flowering trees will in time frame evergreen entry garden that stays neat the year around.*

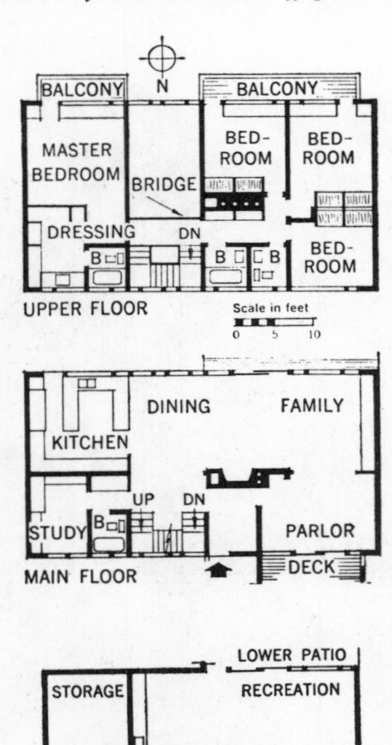

Its back turns to the street

ARCHITECT: LIDDLE AND JONES

When a property-owner builds on the last vacant lot in a well-established section of a city—as in this case in Tacoma—he has to deal with one and possibly two main problems. One is to make the house fit the neighborhood. The other is to find privacy on a street that is likely to have become a thoroughfare in recent years.

In designing this house, architects Liddle and Jones took note of the main traits shared by the houses in the neighborhood: Height and bulk. They placed the main floor a story above the lower level of the lot, and the bedrooms on a third story. Thus they gained valuable garden space, a partially daylit basement, and a house with individuality yet in harmony with its neighbors, built a generation before.

The task of turning the house away from the street was simplified by the lot's location on the south side. The main living and sleeping rooms face south toward sun and warmth.

Landscape architect Robert Chittock designed a fairly tailored, formal street-side garden to help fit the site into its traditional surroundings. In the rear, a tall wall divides the garden into two very distinct areas. The upper terrace was kept simple and restrained for quiet use by adults. The lower level is organized for children's play and for use by the entire family as an outdoor recreation area.

A swimming pool is to be built later. The sideyard is designed to accommodate the heavy excavating equipment that will come to build the pool.

From the back *of the lot you can look down to the play area, or across to a more formal upper terrace (plan below).*

Dining area's *lofty space is a dramatic contrast to lower ceiling in kitchen, which can be closed off by shoji.*

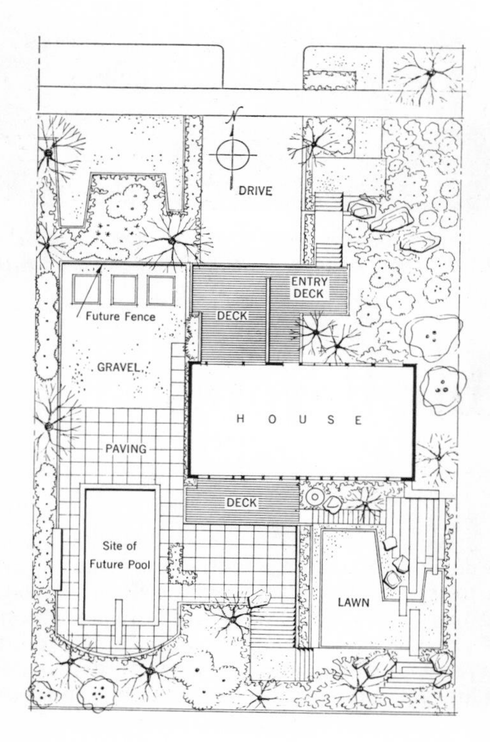

Family life *centers on activities including children, so maximum space went into family room. Beyond fireplace, a formal parlor.*

Double row *of windows indicates two-story living room. Top row helps light recreation room on top level (it is a mezzanine to the living room). Bottom-most windows mark the children's bedrooms. Living room balcony leads to lower terrace (at left).*

A topsy-turvy house...but it works

ARCHITECT: ANTON MUELLER

The kitchen is on the upper level, the living room is a level below that, and the bedrooms are still another level down. The back garden is at the front and the front door is at the back.

This may sound a bit strange, but it works. It is the only way architect Mueller could find to design his house in Bellevue without altering the grade level of his sloping lot, or cutting down two old and very handsome fruit trees, or removing any of the large fir trees that screen the lot along two of its sides.

The level part of the lot at the front is also the sunniest, so it was developed as the main outdoor living area. It is screened from the street by trees, garage, and storage unit. Guests come in over a covered entry bridge along one side of the house to the front door at the back. In effect, they walk by the outdoor sitting area, but not through it. The bridge also provides some privacy from the neighbors on the north side.

Covered bridge *to Bellevue, Wash., house starts at double entry doors between garage and storage room (see plan below, left), then leads past upper level patio to front door at rear. Tree in bloom is one of old cherry trees the owners saved.*

Deck *off family room and kitchen joins level lawn area which is also the sunniest part of the garden. Garden area off master bedroom you see in plan below is actually under deck outside family room. The landscape architect was William Teufel.*

Rooms *at upper level are primarily for daytime activities—dining room, kitchen, family room—to minimize stair climbs. In the evening, the family moves down to the living room for after-dinner activities or for entertaining.*

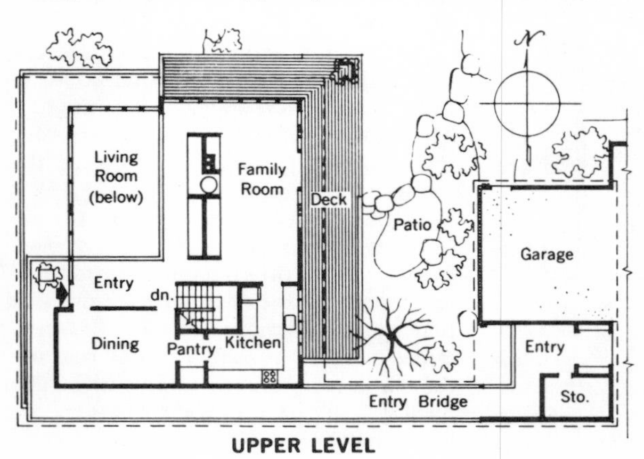

UPPER LEVEL

Balcony
Living Room
Study Guest
dn.
up
B

MIDDLE LEVEL

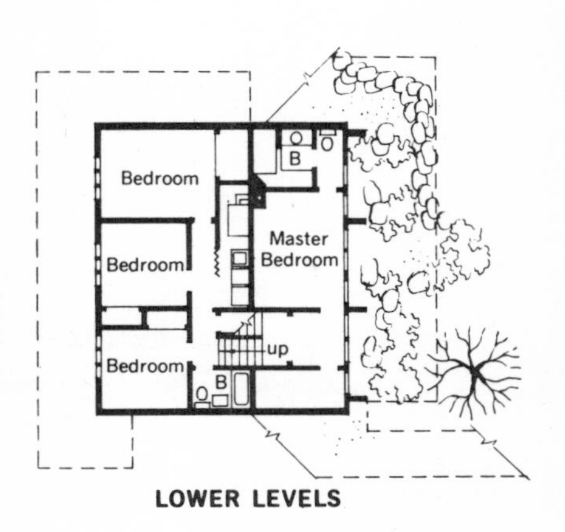

LOWER LEVELS

View *from street shows how house is tucked back into the hill. Concrete walls were sandblasted to expose aggregate.*

This house holds up the

ARCHITECT: CARL MASTON

Plan shows *top floor of 3-story building. Pool, terrace are 16 feet above street.*

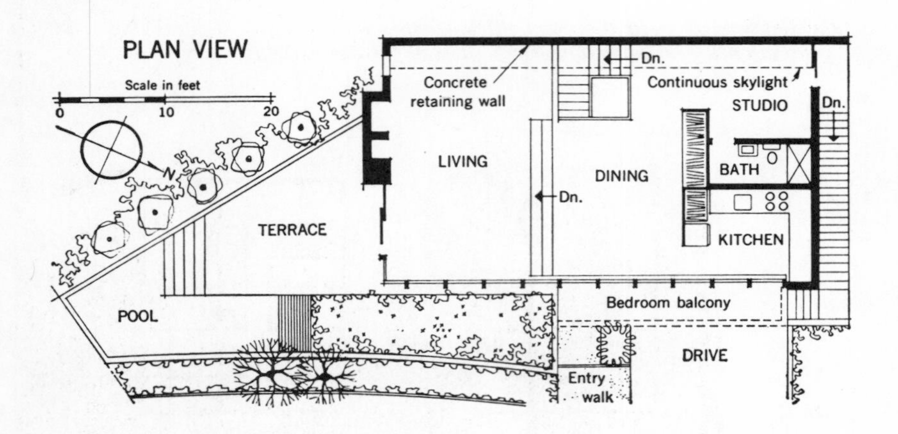

What seemed an impossible building site now holds a three-story concrete house complete with private terrace and swimming pool. It is a fairly common practice in such situations to build on stilts and gain level space by means of decks.

Architect Maston did not wish to use the platform technique for his house in Los Angeles, so it snuggles into the hill. The house itself is designed as a massive retaining wall, leaving the rest of the hill in its natural state.

In this location, the solution is considerably more expensive than a platform. The excavation required amounted to a huge mound of earth. The massive rear wall of the house towers above the street, so building the forms and pouring the concrete were difficult tasks. The results were clearly worth the expense to the owner.

Terrace *is cultivated; hillside above is left untouched.*

Skylight *parallels top of rear (retaining) wall of house.*

hill behind it

Dotted line *indicates the original grade of the hill.*

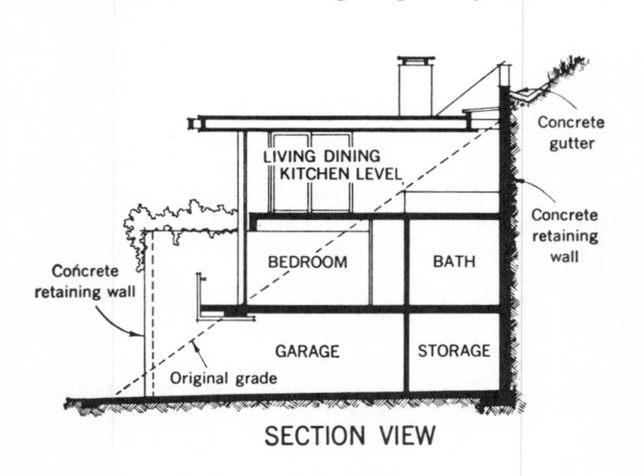

Floors *of acid-resistant brick (no mortar) over electric-heating coils.*

More two-story home plans

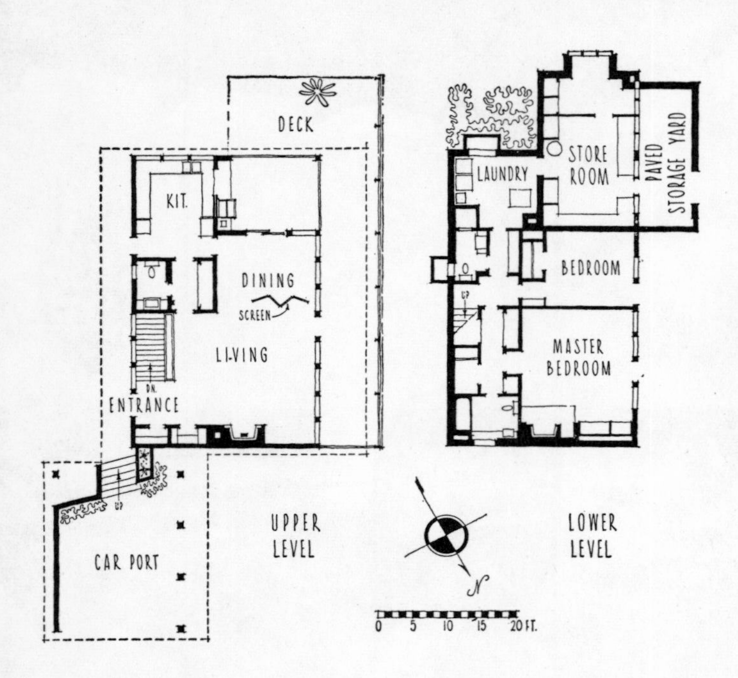

The slope *drops sharply away from the carport end of this house. The result of careful landscape planning and building is a compact two-story building that is closely related to its natural garden surroundings when viewed from the uphill side of the lot—and which yet provides a lofty perch from which to view a vast waterscape spread out to the west. The zoning keeps most maintenance functions on the lower level. The architects were Bain and Overturf.*

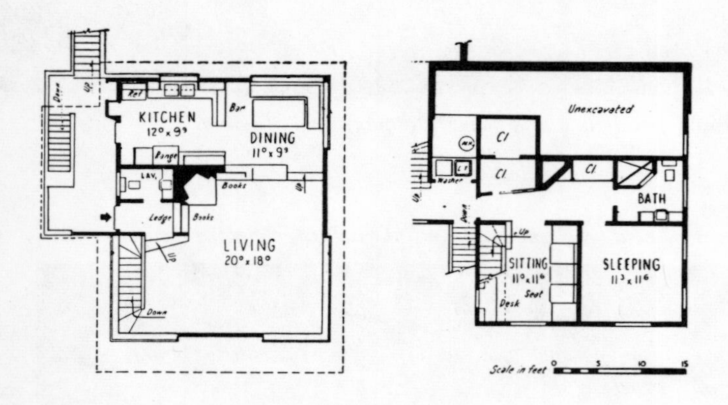

This house *cost an enormous amount of money. It clings by means of massive masonry foundations to a steep, rocky cliff high above the Pacific Ocean. (The living and sleeping rooms look out to sea.) The building is far below the road level, yet the site offered such great rewards to its owners that the expense was not a consideration. Designer Nello Zava developed the floor plan to minimize stair traffic.*

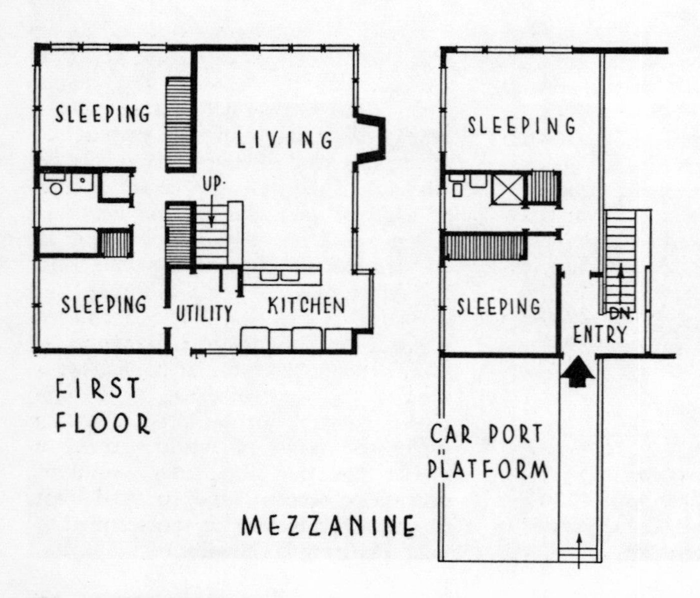

The problems *of the site were: To obtain outdoor living space without building extensive decks (solved, with a terrace off the dining area-kitchen), and to minimize a great deal of climbing on a steep site (solved with a two-story ceiling in the living room and the mezzanine) without altering the natural slope to receive the house. The architects were Schubart and Friedman.*

Unusual Designs

For sheer drama, the house on stilts is as satisfactory a design as contemporary architecture has to offer to the average homebuyer.

Living rooms in mid-air, at tree-top level or higher, possess an air of excitement that is hard to match.

Platform construction has its practical merits, too. In most cases, stilts eliminate altogether the need to excavate. On steeply pitched sites this goes beyond convenience; it is even an out-and-out necessity on some extreme slopes.

Stories of houses shown on this page are to be found: top photo, page 40; next photo, page 42; third photo, page 43; and bottom photo, page 38.

Post-and-pier construction is advisable where there is expansive soil (the kind of clay that shrinks and cracks when it dries) that will not support a continuous foundation. In earthquake zones, this kind of construction is often advisable if the posts can be set in caps of concrete anchored to solid bedrock. There are other advantages noted in the section on construction methods, beginning on p 122.

But all is not roses. The open area beneath the floor requires extra insulation. In some brush fire areas, fire codes require the underpinnings to be enclosed, to stop fire drafts from getting under the house. If utilities make a clutter on the underside, neighbors downslope become annoyed. And some of your friends may be too terrified to visit. Planning is the solution.

From road, *added wing appears to hover in trees. Clean appearance of carport achieved by use of edge-laminated 2 by 4's.*

The living room is perched in the tree tops

ARCHITECT: JOHN FIELD

Side view *shows steepness of the slope.*

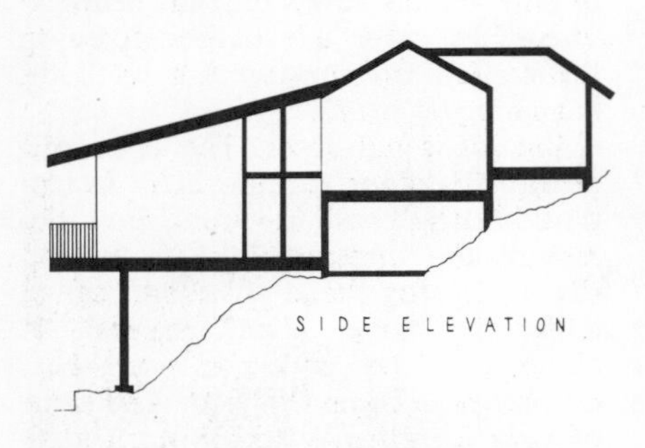

Once a summer cabin, this house became a spacious and thoroughly comfortable year-around home with the addition of a spacious living room on stilts.

The owner's first idea was to add a room on the downhill side, at the existing floor level. However, the architect realized that this would diminish a marvelous view of the valley below. So he designed a more economical addition, taking its level from the existing basement footings. Set down among the treetops the new living room exploits downward, outward, and upward views (of valley, bay, and mountains), which seem greater in depth because of foreground trees.

While the building is a remodeled one, it is an excellent example of the freedom to be gained through use of platform construction on precipitous sites. The addition required little grading; it allowed the house to break free of the contour in order to make better use of views, and careful design of understructures produced an appearance from below that is graceful and free of unsightly utility pipes and the like.

From first *terrace above street, living room appears this way.*

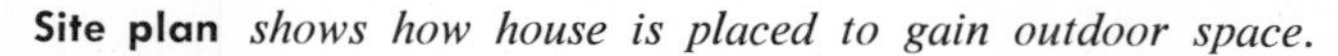

Site plan *shows how house is placed to gain outdoor space.*

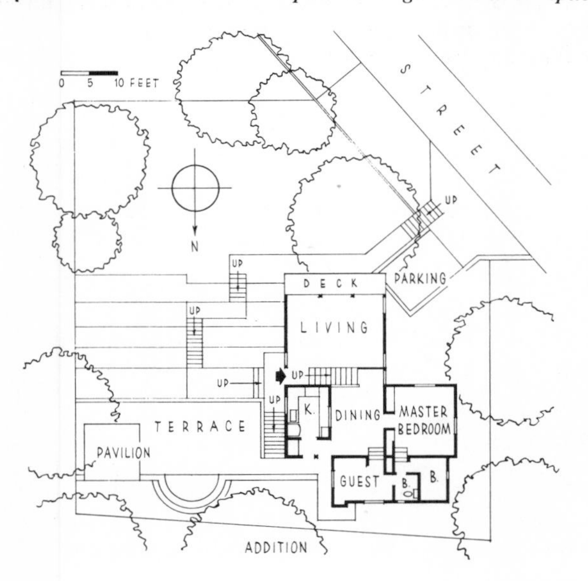

Dining room *looks down to living room, shares view of bay.*

Kitchen, *dining room are linked by closable pass-through.*

Tree-house *quality of living room revealed in this view.*

Concrete piers *lift this Seattle hillside house up off the ground so that all rooms can be located on one floor. The driveway swings up under the bedroom wing, providing sheltered entrance to the house (see side view, below).*

Built in mid-air to gain a sense of space

ARCHITECT: TUCKER, SHIELDS & TERRY

Here is a one-floor house built on piers from the highest point on its hillside site. Besides the convenience of having all the rooms on one floor, the owners wanted their house high enough so they could see out over the dense growth of native trees to a fine view of Seattle.

A sensation of open space is created by the long gallery hallway in the bedroom wing and by the sweep of unbroken space between the master bedroom and the living room-dining room. By opening the sliding doors at each end of the study (see floor plan), the owners can lie in bed and watch a fire in the living room fireplace or look out through the dining room window wall almost 50 feet away.

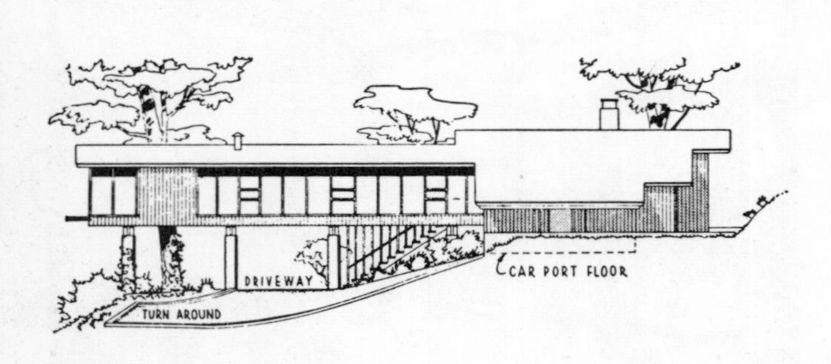

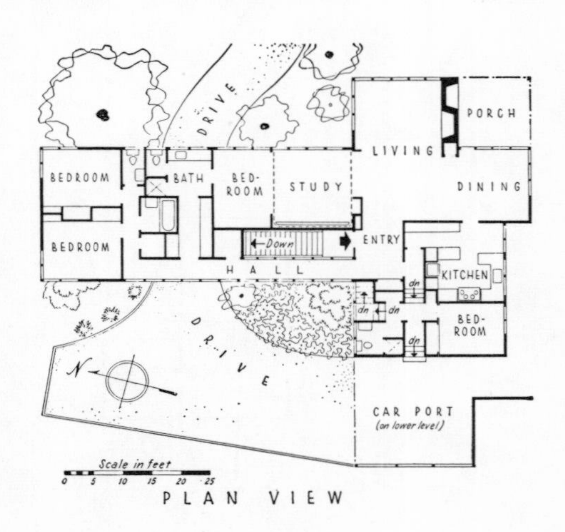

Outdoor porch *off the dining room has a fireplace to take away the chill on cool evenings. Fireplace also serves as barbecue.*

Living room *looks out over Lake Washington. Wood paneling of walls is vertical grain, tongue and groove cedar.*

View *from bedroom into study. Sliding doors permit study to extend either bedroom or living room.*

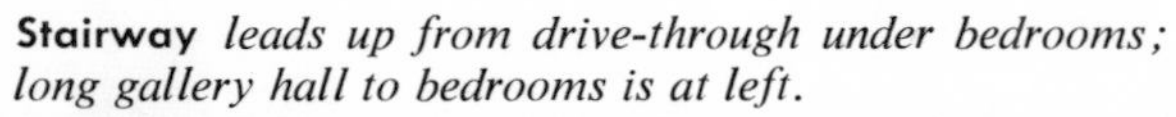

Stairway *leads up from drive-through under bedrooms; long gallery hall to bedrooms is at left.*

View *of bedroom wing from carport. Windows of long gallery hall are shaded by split bamboo blinds that let in some light.*

House *appears to grow out of a rocky ridge in the hills near Boise, Ida. The basically circular structure of the house takes fullest advantage of sweeping views, and the deck off the dining room brings owners even closer to their view.*

It's cantilevered...to soar above the view

ARCHITECT: ARTHUR L. TROUTNER

This hilltop house awakens a flood of exciting associations: The cave, the castle in the crags, the lookout tower. It soars above an immense view, but it has a certain feeling of intimacy and solidity that ties it securely to earth.

The owner-designer purposely chose the spectacular but difficult site. His solution to the problem of perching a house on this ridge determined the form of the house: It is a 16-sided polygon with floors cantilevered from a central steel support. A great wall built of weathered, lichen-encrusted rock gathered from the site helps stabilize the structure and also pleases the eye.

Despite the steep slope, the house has generous usable outdoor areas. They float as cantilevered decks, or nestle as stone-paved terraces.

The circular form offers economy of circulation space, concentrated in the center, and off which rooms open in wedge shapes. This economy is offset, however, by the need for special carpentry work to fit the sloping, tapering framing of the house.

The site's final dividend is natural air-conditioning by up and down-valley breezes, channeled through the windows.

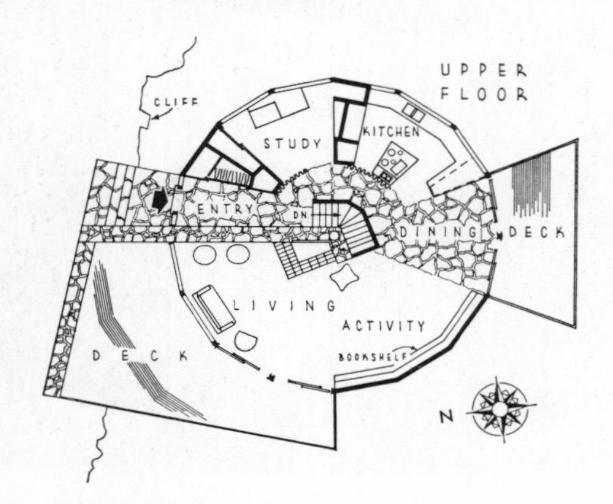

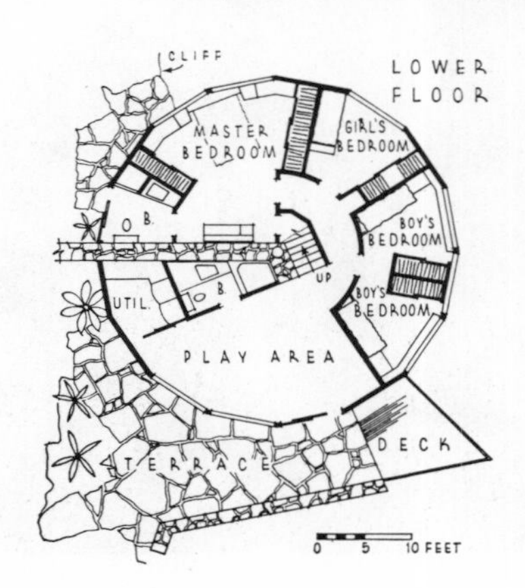

Floor *of dining area is paved with local stone, a more finely quarried selection of the same type used in the wall (see below). Kitchen windows have full view, made opener by locations of pass-throughs and open storage cabinets.*

Living room. *Massive rock wall's solidity balances openness of house. The radial beams of the 16-sided house are 2 by 14's. Lighter members repeat wedge-shaped design factor in rooms on lower level, reached by stair at near end of stone wall.*

Fireplace, *at one end of living room, consists of a metal hood mounted to wall covered with quarry tile. Flooring is exposed aggregate. Usual masonry fireplace and chimney would have posed weight problem, required some excavation, added to cost.*

To keep a natural slope, they put the house

ARCHITECT: MARQUIS AND STOLLER

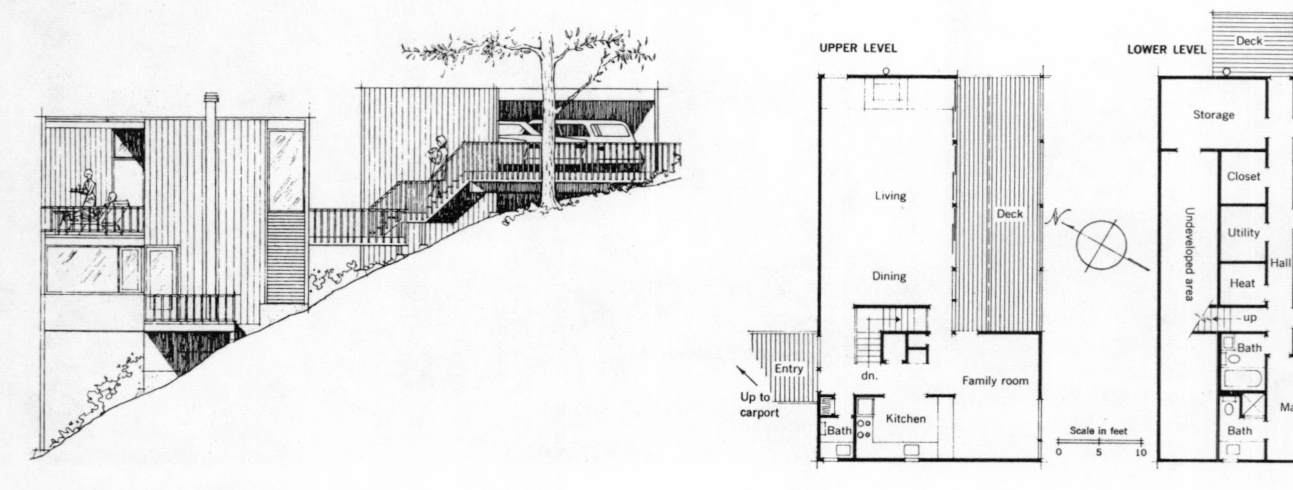

Other end *of living room has dining area; stairs to lower level are behind wall. Entry hall at right; hall to kitchen and family room, left. Adjustable gallery-type fixtures, mounted on a continuous track on ceiling, light paintings on wall at right.*

up on stilts

Building on a hillside can be an expensive venture, but there are ways to balance out some of the extra costs.

The house shown here, for example, was designed by architects Marquis and Stoller to take advantage of the existing grade on a site in Mill Valley, Calif. No excavation was required, and no costly retaining walls. To avoid digging into the hill for the lower floor, the architects simply pushed it forward (see sketch of side-view) and used part of its roof for the main outdoor living deck. Costs were also held down by using a boxlike construction with a simple framing system. But a high ceiling and the extension of roof beams over the deck keep the living room from seeming boxlike.

Kitchen *and bathroom behind it are directly over two bathrooms below, to cut costs and concentrate weight on the uphill side. This approach simplifies plumbing problems.*

More unusual designs

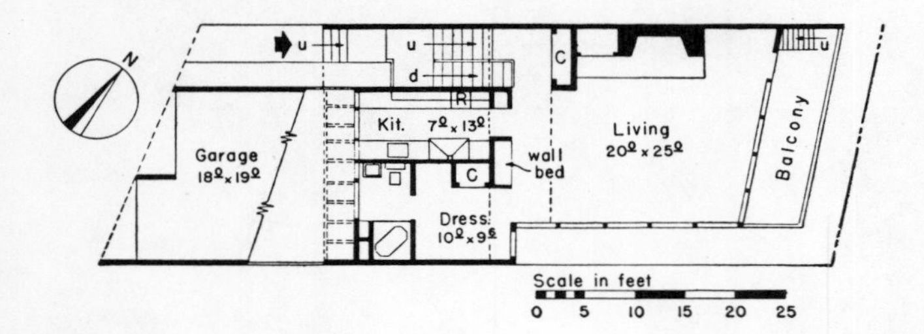

On a steep lot *in San Francisco, platform construction was the only answer. It got the living areas of the house up to enjoy the view of the bay at relatively little cost. An intermediate level entry connects the living areas with the carport, and also leads down to a lower level—the stilts were enclosed to form a recreation room. This room can be remodeled to any purpose if the owners so wish. Architect was John Elkin Dinwiddie.*

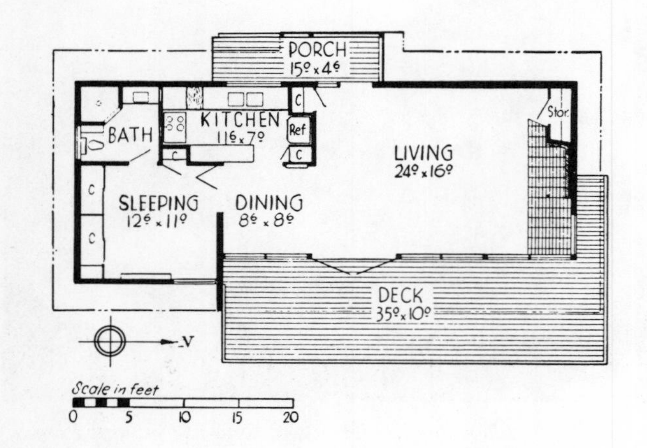

On a steep slope, *this house manages to blend into the contour of the hill. From above, a blank wall is coupled with a flat roof to present a low silhouette. On the downhill side, below a cantilevered deck, the posts are covered with diagonal sheathing which is painted a dark brown. The architect planned this lower space so that it can be finished for lower-level rooms later if the need arises. Architects: Campbell & Wong.*

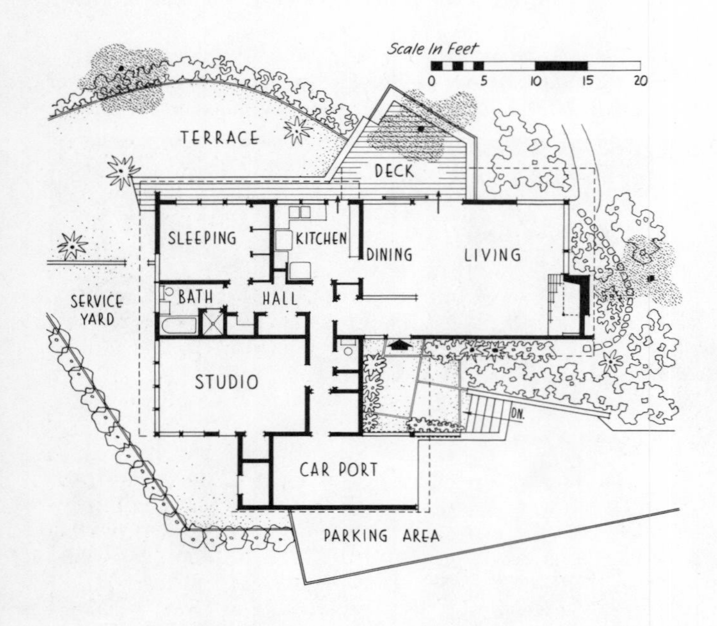

Another house *by the designers of the one shown above shows differences imposed by a differing terrain. In this case, the living room end of the house is poised above a grade that slopes away in two directions. The deck is built around mature trees to preserve their shade value. The need for a carport forced outdoor living space onto a terraced area below the house, and onto the deck. The studio is intentionally separated from the bedroom and living room.*

Hill-hugging Homes

Following the contour—stringing the house out along the face of the slope—is a favorite design technique of architects and homeowners who want the house to fit into its site with a minimum of fuss.

Where the lot is on the high side of the street, this kind of site-hugging makes the house seem easier to approach. Long, low houses downslope from the street interfere less with the view beyond, and so seem more a part of it. Where there is still a rural flavor, or one of wilderness, the long, low house does not stick out so obtrusively.

The basic quality of such homes is that their rooms tend to fall all in a line, and in this they resemble the classic Western ranch house. Careful "zoning" of activities allows great privacy in homes of this type. Children can raise a particular ruckus without causing undue discomfort to their elders, providing their quarters are distantly separated from a den or master bedroom.

Shallow slopes pose fewer problems in landscaping for outdoor living, because patios or terraces can go on one side or the other of the house. The long line of the structure seldom permits floor level terraces at either end, sometimes the only choice on a steeply sloping site.

Stories of houses shown on this page are to be found: top photo, page 56; next photo, page 52; third photo, page 48; and bottom photo, page 58.

Sitting area *is daylit by high clerestory window, and is a part of the family room-dining area. Doors at left open to the terrace. This view is from the hall leading to the bedrooms toward the entry, which is beyond plastic screen.*

A house built for a shrinking family

ARCHITECT: TERRY AND MOORE

The requirements for designing a house for a shrinking family are just as exacting as the requirements for designing a house for an expanding family.

Here is shown the house one woman built after three of her four children had grown and left home. It was designed to accommodate a teen-age daughter still living at home, and a college stusent son who spends his weekends at home.

For this family situation, the big two-story house the children grew up in was no longer necessary. The new house could be small, and more outward turning (to the garden the owner was now free to develop and tend as a hobby).

It was now feasible to place the master bedroom in a private situation, at the opposite end of the house from the other two bedrooms. These bedrooms are close to the kitchen, family room, terrace, and utility room. They form an apartment-like unit, separate from the master bedroom and living room side of the house, for the children when they return for visits.

The house, designed by architects Terry and Moore, was carefully planned to exploit the hillside site on the shore of Lake Washington, and detailed to shift emphasis to adults' rather than children's needs.

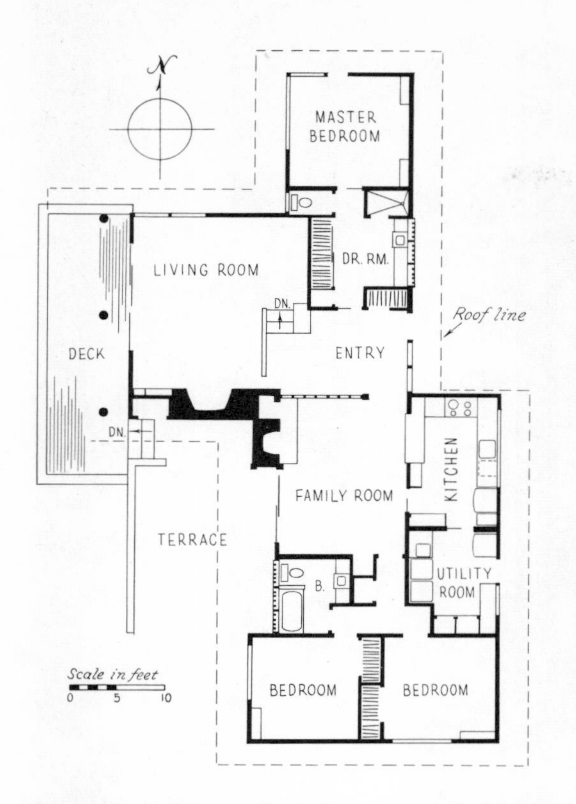

Floor plan *of house shows how master bedroom is separated from other bedroom wing. View from lake shore shows living room as dominant feature, with its roofed deck. In the photo, the master bedroom is to the left of the deck area.*

Left. *From the living room, looking back to the entry. Clerestory windows and plastic screen make this area in center of house light during the day.* **Below,** *kitchen, which is parallel to family room, and which can be closed off by pull-down door.*

Fireplace *in living room outlined by wood framing, relating masonry to wood finish of room. The shape of the fireplace repeats the shape of the living room window at opposite end of the room (the window above the garage).*

It nestles on a wooded, sloping hillside

ARCHITECT: HARWELL HAMILTON HARRIS

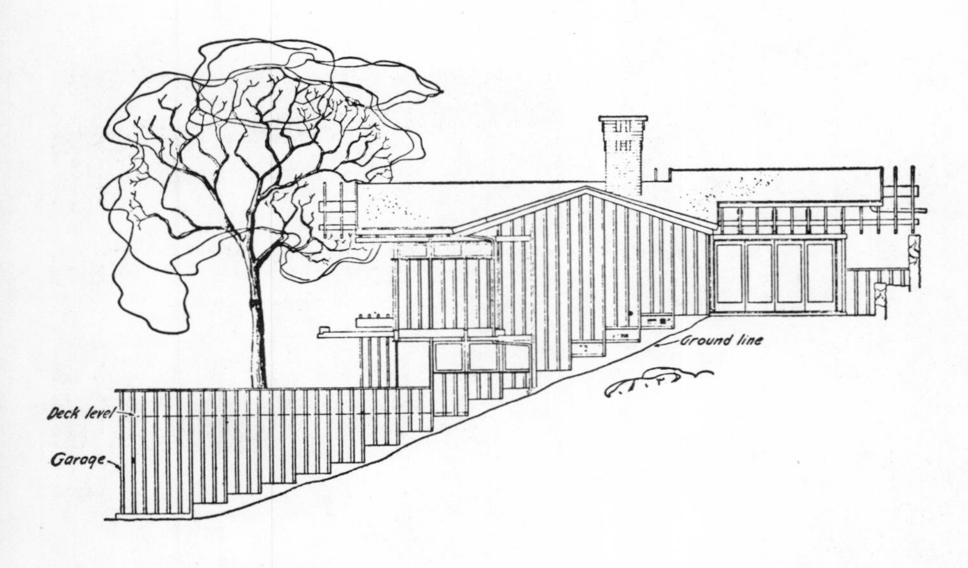

This graceful house, nested like a living thing in its natural setting, achieves two outdoor living areas on a relatively steep slope.

One bedroom above the garage opens directly on a private sundeck at the front of the house. The room, studio-like, has a separate entry and can be used as a private apartment. It is the only room below the main floor level.

All other rooms, on the floor above, have easy access to a rear patio carved out of the wooded hillside. Although this patio is out of doors, it gives a great feeling of shelter. It is surrounded on two sides by the house. Its third side is the hill which is bulwarked by a masonry retaining wall. The fourth side is a glass and lath plant shelter. Overhead, the regular roof rafters provide some sense of protection without hiding handsome trees and the sky from view.

Designer Harris made both areas contribute effectively to the harmony between house and site.

Built-in *book case covers one wall of living room. Ceiling is combed plywood.*

Entry *is along rear wall of fireplace. Passage at left leads to living room.*

Garage *set forward on hillside lot gives privacy from the street. Sun deck over garage adjoins small studio below main floor of the house.*

From end *of entry hall, view is out to patio, which is enclosed by extensions of house beams and rafters.*

Floor plan *shows how house wraps around downslope side of patio to complete seclusion. Ramp leads up rock wall.*

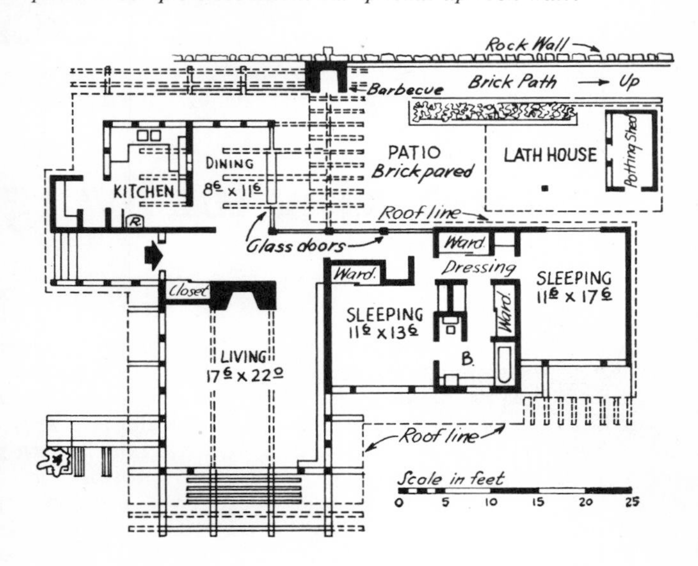

In living room, *dropped ceiling section over sitting area has a comfortable, sheltering effect to contrast with high, daylit space beyond. The deck extends the apparent room size while its solid rail edits the view in favor of the hills.*

One wing for living...one for sleeping

ARCHITECT: ROGER LEE

One of the most attractive qualities of this sloping lot is a spur of mountains several miles off to the southeast. The house is designed to get full value from the view without exposing the owners too much to the hot summer sun.

Architect Lee organized the building into two clearly separated areas, for living and sleeping. A central hall makes it possible to move easily and directly from the entry to any of the rooms. A deck that begins at grade level in front and ends at grade level in the rear extends this level as an outdoor living area around the downslope half of the house, and provides an outdoor route for moving between rooms.

The uphill side of the house, facing the street, is almost blank except for some high windows. The solid rail of the deck combines with this face to give the house privacy from the street without blocking the larger view. The living-dining-kitchen block of the house creates a secluded eating area on the deck, part open and part under louvered shade, and all handy to the kitchen.

The plan was formed to facilitate the adding of another bedroom at some future time.

Street facade *is private except for living room windows above the deck rail. House seems to nestle into slope.*

Well-lighted *entry guides visitors from carport to door. Translucent plastic screen conceals a service yard.*

At night. *Living area wing creates privacy for deck, including lattice-shaded eating area outside kitchen.*

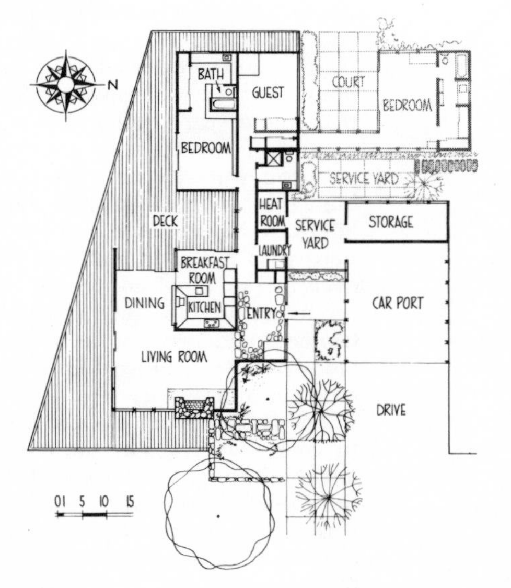

Study *is equipped for guest sleeping. It looks out on floor-level rear garden; gets added light from high windows.*

Long narrow *house rides above concrete masonry foundation wall. Open stairways lead from decks down to patio built on the basement floor of a structure removed long before this house was built. Stream flows beneath bridge at right.*

Construct a sturdy masonry pedestal

ARCHITECT: BUFF, STRAUB & HENSMAN

In nearly every town and city there are still unusual building sites that were overlooked in the rush to find a conventional level lot—one on which the prospective homeowner could easily visualize his house.

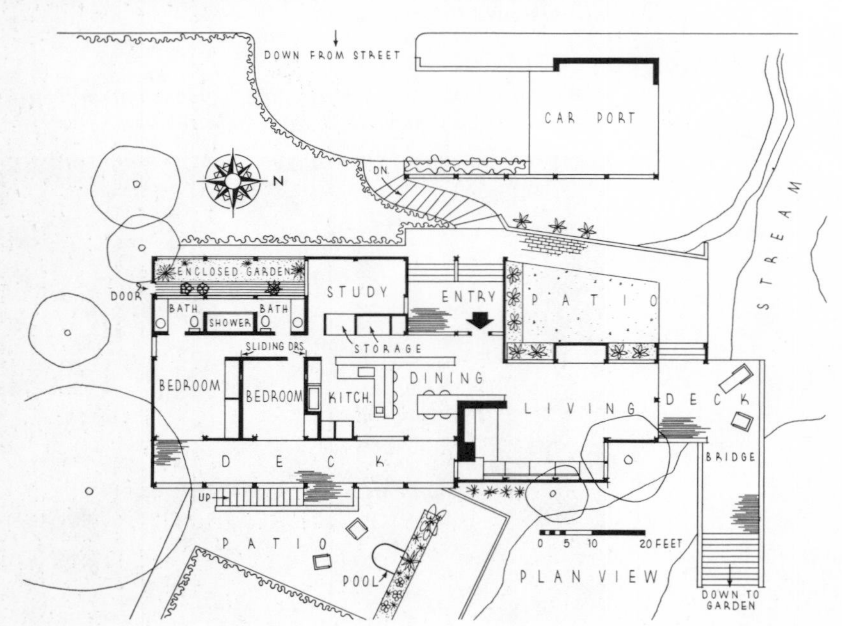

One fortunate couple found just such a site, a remainder of an older Pasadena estate that had been overlooked by many other home-builders. However, the couple was not sure of the find until they showed the lot to architects Buff, Straub, and Hensman, who spotted the potentialities and proceeded to design this house to take advantage of the lovely trees and a year-around stream.

Study the photographs and floor plan, and you will see how the house was built right over its unusual site, downhill from the street and over the foundations of a previous building. A bridge over the stream leads from the living room terrace to the garden below. Closed space inside a narrow concrete block pedestal is utilized for storage and mechanical utilities.

The prime objective of the design was to gain livability. For the owners, the long built-in sofa with its bookcase, and the raised hearth are outstanding successes. The utility of the bathroom is more than matched by the attractiveness that stems from its private garden.

Arrangement *of generous-sized fireplace, bookshelf wall, and built-in sofa creates a warm, inviting atmosphere in the long living room. A wall at right of fireplace screens this room from entry. Window wall is opposite the fireplace.*

Bathtub-shower *is recessed in floor, and lined with granite-finish tile.*

Translucent *plastic screen encloses garden outside the bath. Door provides access from outside. Shower separates twin bath facilities (doors off for photo).*

Here is how *house is set into wooded hillside. Deck is set to one side of dining room windows to retain view from them. The photograph was taken before foreground area was landscaped with a variety of small flowering trees and shrubs.*

Discreetly fitted against a wooded hill

ARCHITECT: DEWITT C. ROBINSON

The natural site was altered very little for this house in Oswego Skylands, 10 miles south of Portland. The house nestles just below the brow of a wooded knoll, at the feet of stately Douglas firs, and almost every room has a magnificent view of the Willamette River several hundred feet below, and the majestic Mount Hood several miles away.

The house design capitalizes on its surroundings. The roof has a gentle pitch, so the house seems to hug the hill. The exterior siding was left its natural color to blend in with the soil and meadows. Gray-green panels by the entry pick up the foliage color of the Douglas firs.

If you look at the plan at right, you will see that the house structure encloses a court. However, this is not an inward-turning house with main views toward the court and outdoor living concentrated there. Living areas of the house really face the river scene. Visitors enter through the court, then become aware of the orientation toward the view as they encounter in rapid succession the huge windows of the living room, and the deck off the dining room, where the owners entertain, enjoy breakfast or lunch, soak up the morning sun, or just sit and admire their view. (The deck is set over in front of the kitchen to preserve the view from the dining room.)

The master bedroom faces into the hill and cool shade of the Douglas firs. Its terrace can be shut off for privacy or thrown open to the inner court merely by opening or closing double doors in the wall of the covered entry walk. Since the doors are covered with the same siding as the wall they are hardly noticeable when closed.

Solid panels alternate with slatted panels to separate the drive from the patio and entry court. The solid panels keep the house interior hidden from arrivals in the driveway. The slatted panels make the court seem open to persons looking out from the house or the patio.

The huge garden has some selected plantings to supplement the natural growth of the area; otherwise only the patio area has an appreciable amount of cultivated plant material. A barbecue is in a clearing away from the house.

Entry walk *is roofed over for comfort of rainy-season visitors.*

Inner court *is change-of-pace view. Entry walk is at left in photo.*

Living room *is three steps lower than study and entrance hall (see plan). Snow-clad mountain is framed in center window above stand of Douglas fir.*

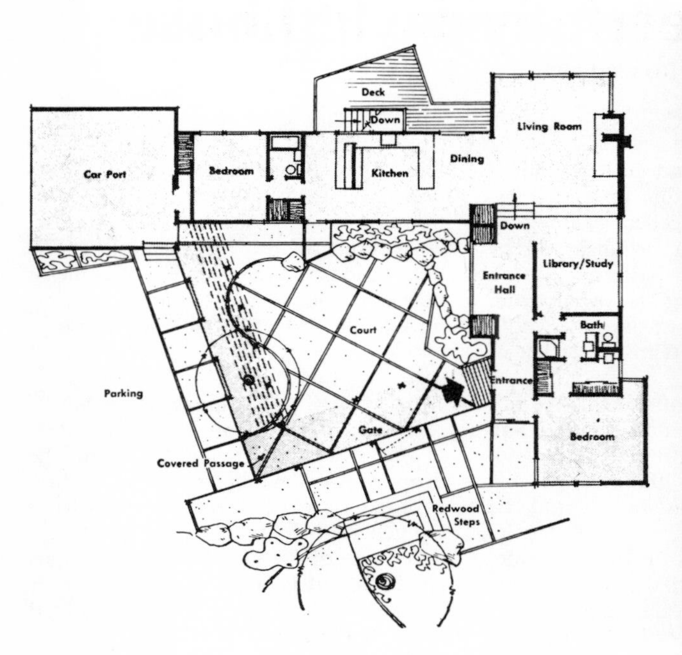

Private patio *is just off master bedroom. Double doors at right can be opened to connect it to the inner court. Steps lead to path.*

House *is set forward on narrow shelf to provide space for ground level outdoor living between building, retaining wall.*

The shed roof shields windows on the west; east light enters through clerestory windows and window wall below.

A cheerfully daylit house

ARCHITECT: ROGER LEE

Future *plans call for wing extending bedroom end of house toward slope.*

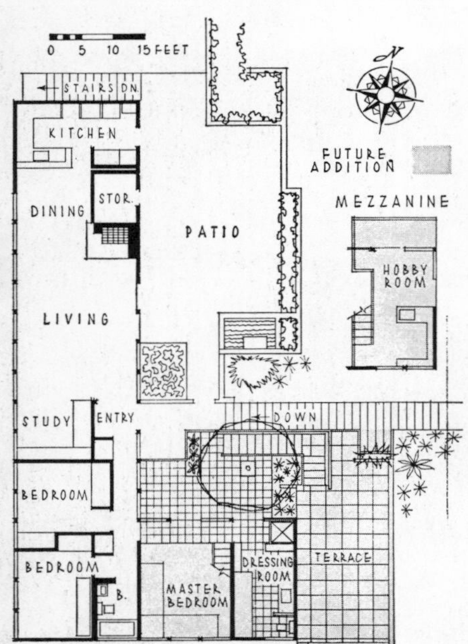

The soft flood of balanced light that is an integral part of this long, narrow house makes it an excellent example of how to use daylight in a hillside home (or any other for that matter).

From the beginning the owners and architect Lee knew that daylight would play an important part in the design of the house.

They wanted, of course, to take advantage of a spectacular view of San Francisco Bay (the site is in Berkeley), but they realized that the glare of sky, water, and afternoon sun would be a problem.

To reduce the glare on the view side, the roof slopes down like a vizor outside the windows, and the glass does not go all the way to the floor. To balance this band of bright light, there are floor-to-ceiling windows and high clerestory windows on the opposite side of the house. As a result there is a high level of daylight inside, and the problem of contrast between indoors and outdoors is minimized. The generous and careful use of windows opens up the interior so it seems light and airy.

As with all good things, there can be too much, so the architect added a study at one end of the living room, and he dropped the ceiling to make a dim, cave-like retreat that offers a relief from the general brightness of the house.

Because of the glass, the house seems larger than it is, a spacious feeling that is especially fortunate in a house planned for later expansion.

Living room, *looking toward study with its cave-like quality beneath section of dropped ceiling. Sliding doors in window wall at left lead out to patio. Windows at right look out on limitless view. Bedrooms, bath down hall behind study.*

Intimate patio *between house and slope is concrete, with a generous planting bed just outside the window wall.*

Dining room *displays one delightful aspect of high windows—view into tree tops. Storage in wall behind the fireplace.*

More hill-hugging home plans

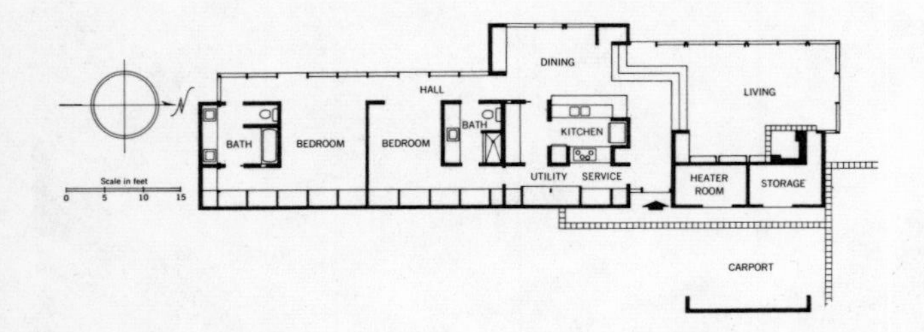

This entire house *faces a view to the west. It is small, but seems spacious because of its glass wall on the view side, and its 80 foot length. The house backs right up to the street, to maximize the level space on the view side, to allow a swimming pool. The glass wall is shaded by a wide overhang, by bamboo blinds that drop vertically from the outer edge of the overhang, and by bamboo in containers all along the wall. The architects were Holmes and Sellery.*

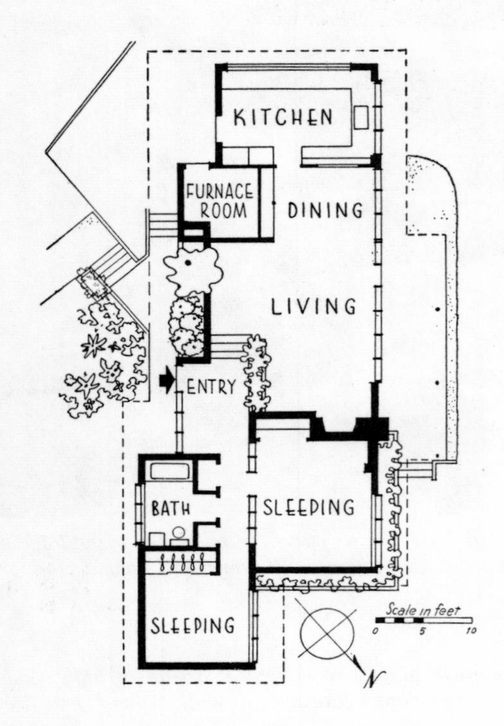

On a pie-shaped *and steep site, this house snuggles down between two low retaining walls, to look out over a lake. The view is to the northwest, and every room shares in it. The offset second bedroom maximizes the view for each of the bedrooms. On a level below the house, there is a small roofed shelter for beach parties and barbecues, and there is a small boat dock. The architect was Ross Copeland, Jr.*

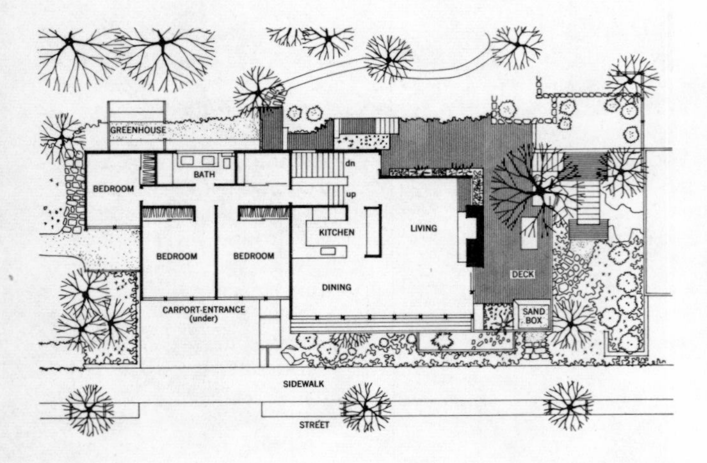

The garden *was planted by the owners, who lowered themselves on ropes after the fashion of mountain climbers. That gives you an idea how steep the lot is. The street side is the downhill side. Amazingly, the view from the living room is an intimate one of the garden, which is designed to be close to eye level wherever the eye goes. Decks are almost the only outdoor living area, so easy circulation of traffic was the main aim of the floor plan. Architect, James E. Hussey.*

Design Details

There are matters of detail that should occupy the attentions of a hillside home buyer to a considerable degree.

A man who wants to live on the flat can ignore some of them altogether, or pay scant attention to the rest.

A man who wants to live on the flat can screen out an excess of summer sun with an inexpensive patio screen in no time at all, or with a line of fast-growing trees in a matter of a year or so. His hillside counterpart, with windows 20 feet above grade level, must devote himself to the problem more earnestly. The earlier he does so, the less costly will be the cure.

Housekeeping on the flat is not an easy task, but at least it doesn't involve carting the laundry, the vacuum, and the groceries up and down stairs.

This section offers some helpful hints on how to get around these problems, to say nothing of putting those lofty windows within reach of suds and a squeegee.

If hillside homes impose these difficulties, they also offer the opportunity to use dramatic stairways in living rooms or entry halls. Stairs are often necessary in hillside homes, but pages 66 through 69 demonstrate that they need not be merely so—that they can lend special drama while serving their purpose.

The stories connected with the photos are to be found as follows: top photo, page 63; next photo, page 70; third photo, page 66; and bottom photo, page 65.

Beating the climate on exposed slopes

Climate control is one of the most important factors in designing (or remodeling) a great many hillside homes.

On view sites, especially where the view is toward the setting sun, the view side of the house is often primarily of glass. Glass is among the least efficient insulators.

View or no view, the sun and wind are less obstructed on slopes than they are on the flat, so houses get less natural insulation. This is because air is almost always in motion on a slope, rising as it warms and descending as it cools. If the house blocks its passage in either direction, climate control devices have to compensate. Still another point is that the upslope side of a house can be dim for lack of adequate daylight unless some special measures are taken.

Architects and designers have excellent answers to all of these problems. Some of the most widely-used methods are noted here.

Window walls and sun

Blocking the sun before it reaches the glass is six times more effective for cooling than stopping it once it has come through, as with draperies or blinds.

Horizontal sunshades—extended eaves or roofs over decks—predominate. They do not interfere with views. They let in late afternoon (or early morning) and winter sun. They do not have to be maneuvered every day.

Horizontal shades are less commonly used because they have the opposite effects in the connections listed above. Sometimes, however, they are necessary and even desirable.

Some flexible ideas for screening are shown on these pages.

High windows and skylights

When a house is built close against an upslope, or when it is cut into its site, the result is often at least one dark, gloomy room—unless the designer makes use of high windows, skylights, or some even more specialized device.

Clerestory windows serve well in many situations, but especially where

Climate control: *1, overhang for shade and rain shelter; 2, screening for insects and blowing dust; 3, canvas on wires for shade; 4, louvered shutters; 5, plastic for breeze control. The overhead beams were planned with other elements in mind.*

Planters *on outside of deck darken it, and tie it to wooded slope below. It is delightful spot for breakfast.*

Openings *in overhang allow sun to penetrate master bedroom with an ideal southeast exposure. Kitchen & Hunt, architects.*

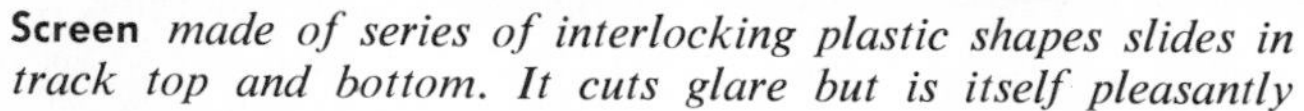

Screen *made of series of interlocking plastic shapes slides in track top and bottom. It cuts glare but is itself pleasantly luminous. When retracted, as shown at lower left, it is hardly visible next to corner posts of roof.*

Unusual planting *of Pittosporum phillyraeoides in deep, 4-foot planting boxes provides natural filter against afternoon sun. The landscape architects were Eckbo, Royston & Williams.*

Canvas *lashed to pipe frames provides summer sun screen for this house. In winter, the frames retract into the soffit, out of view. Designer was Adrian Malone.*

Wire glass *skylight runs from one end of this roof to the other, including the overhang at each end. From outside, it is low and unobtrusive.*

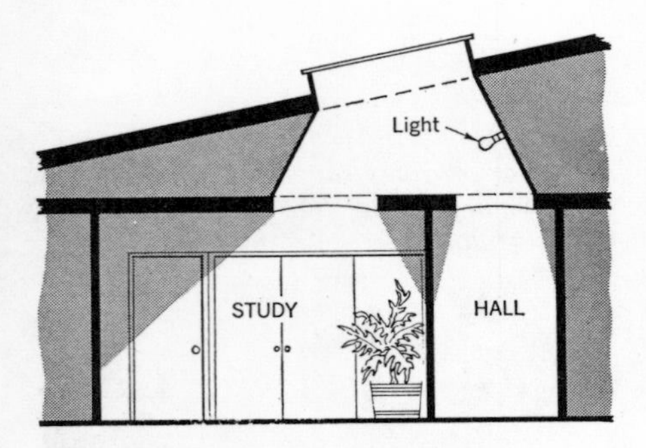

One skylight *and two ceiling domes will light two interior rooms.*

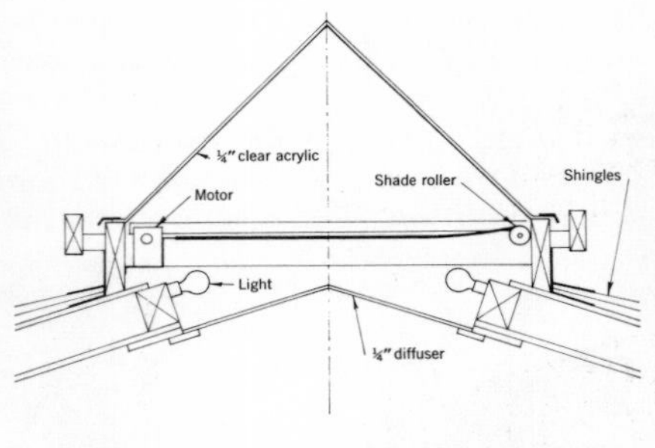

Amount *of light can be controlled with shade devices.*

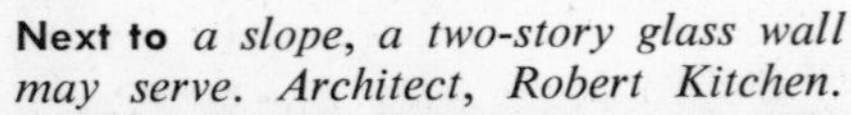

Next to *a slope, a two-story glass wall may serve. Architect, Robert Kitchen.*

Slanting windows *allow extra light in below-grade room. G. Bentley, architect.*

they can balance the light from a window wall—without being exposed themselves to afternoon sun in summer. This type of window at the top of a high wall will let out considerable accumulated heat. (This factor is not all boon where winter mornings are often frosty. Shade devices help in this case.)

Windows high under gables do similar service. For other examples, see homes pictured on pp 18, 28, 52, and 58.

Where windows are not the answer, one or more skylights may be. Skylights are sold in literally dozens of sizes, shapes, and models. Some are built to cut down light and heat; others are built to gain as much of each as possible. Some are vented. Some are hinged so they double as ports leading onto the roof. Some are designed to fit atop light wells with mechanical shades that close off the bottom of the well, giving their owners a choice in amounts of light and heat admitted.

Typical small skylights are made of acrylic plastic, in flush or protruding shapes within the rough size range of 14 by 14 inches up to 46 by 46 inches. Wire glass and ridge units can be bought in sections to make up as long a skylight as you wish. Costs range from about $20 all the way to $500 for manufactured units. Custom jobs may run as high as $2,500.

Skylights pick up only light that falls directly on the face. Flat units pick up less than dome or pyramid shapes. Tilting the face of a skylight to the north also cuts down on the amount of light it gathers (and at the same time cuts down on the amount of heat).

One of the continuing problems in using a skylight is condensation. Some models have double domes; the dead air space between serves as an insulating device to cut down on condensation. Almost all types have gutters built into the unit. Extreme variations in daily temperatures cause the greatest problem (mountain areas, for example), and thus persons living in such areas should pay particular heed to solving the problem by choosing a model that resists condensation.

It is not easy to find skylights for browsing purposes. Best bets are stores that sell window glass, or telephone calls to firms that advertise custom work or to manufacturer's representatives.

Insulation . . . plain and fancy

Houses on exposed sites are almost always served well by insulation even in the mildest of climates.

The more exposed the house is, the

more true the broad statement. It reaches its logical limit with the house on stilts, which must have good insulation in its floor to be a comfortable dwelling. This is because the floor is no different than a wall of a house on ordinary continuous foundations. (Also, many platform homes are most economically heated by forced air systems with ducting in the floor plenum, adding to the necessity.)

There are no automatic advantages in one type of insulation over another just because a house is on a hill. The determining factor is the type of construction, and the wall covering material. Here are the basic types:

Loose fill. It consists of particles, granules, or fibrous materials which are poured or blown into place. Applying loose fill in a finished wall is usually a job for a professional since the material must fill every part of the wall.

Flexible insulation. It is usually made from similar materials to those noted above. It is manufactured in short sections and in continuous rolls. Rolls come in 16, 20, and 24-inch widths to fit between framing members. Thicknesses range from ½-inch to 6 inches. Flexible insulation is usually faced on one side with a vapor barrier material, which should face the interior of the house. It goes up easiest during construction.

Rigid insulation. It comes in the form of structural panels ranging from 2 by 8 feet to 4 by 12 feet. It ranges in thickness from ½ inch to 3 inches, and is made of expanded plastic foams or weightier fibrous pressed board. Types with special finishes can be used in open-beam ceilings where no other type of insulation can be used.

Reflective insulation. It is usually a foil, with either a dead air space in between two sheets of foil, or with one of the mass materials as a core. This material is particularly effective in ceilings when the main problem is resisting summer heat gain.

In most cases, the first half inch thickness of insulating material is the most effective, and two to three inches is an ideal total thickness. Exceptions occur in air-conditioned and electrically heated homes, where every added thickness of insulation cuts down on the required size of the cooling or heating unit.

Unusual ideas. The photographs show a roof pond and a sod roof. Both are extremely effective insulators. For example, in summer a roof temperature may reach 180°, depending on roof composition and hours of sun. The pond roof may keep that figure as low as 100° when outside air temperatures hover near that mark.

Roof ponds *can be very economical insulation in warm summer areas, since flat roof has to be impervious anyway. Weekly replenishing of water supply is the only need. Can be drained in winter. This pond designed by the owner.*

Sod roof *is fireproof, good insulation, can be aesthetically pleasing. This one on house designed by architect Lionel H. Pries is 8 inches deep, held in place by 2 by 6 "vanes." Impervious membrane underlies. Grass is dwarf rye.*

Open-to-view staircases...

Simple stair *leads to bedroom (high up to catch a view) in home by architect Richard Dennis.*

Stairs are a good deal more difficult to deal with than flat floor is, but they are still the only way to get from one story of a house to the next. Given thought, they can be a dramatic part of a hillside home's living room.

There are practical matters of safety, which Robert Wood Kennedy notes in his book *The House and the Art of its Design*. These include:

Correct proportion of run to rise (municipal building codes set certain limits; see below).

Correct hand rail height.

Hand rails both sides, continuous (honored in the breach as often as the observance).

Sufficient head room.

Adequate lighting both day and night.

The absence of winders.

The absence of shelves and hooks.

No doors near stairs.

No circulation across top of stairs.

No windows high above stairs.

Adequate width between rails.

Floor covering both for traction and resilience.

Three-way light switches top and bottom.

Light color risers to silhouette toys or other obstructions on steps.

Clean lines *of this stair achieved with open risers, slim steel balusters. Each tread is wrapped in a carpet that fits like a glove. Architect was George Rockrise.*

A backdrop *to the dining area, the stairwell lends great sense of height to core of house shown on pages 30-31. Short flights and center openwork achieve the effect.*

...an opportunity to add drama to the house

Adequate length in landings.

Uniform risers throughout the house and grounds.

Where the house is to have young children, the following considerations are primary: Top and bottom landings should be designed to accommodate stout gates. Accordion gates or sliding types work equally well if their locks cannot be picked by toddlers. Of course their surfaces should not present toeholds to experimental climbers.

Balusters (the vertical descenders from handrails) should be no more than 6½ inches apart, edge to edge. These also should avoid tempting toeholds.

The National Building Code prescribes limits of the kind Kennedy mentions on the dimensions of stairways. Stairways must be a minimum of 36 inches wide (this does not include special stairs with no emergency escape function, as the case of spiral stairs demonstrates in the section below). Risers cannot exceed 7¾ inches in height. Treads cannot be less wide than 9 inches. The product of riser height and tread width shall be at least 70 inches, but no more than 75 inches. (So, for example, a riser 7 inches high and a tread 10 inches wide make a product of 70 inches, the minimum.)

The national code requires handrails on one side only if the stairs are less than 44 inches in width. If they are wider than 44 inches, handrails should be installed on each side.

Landings must be as long and as wide as the width of the stair.

No flight of stairs between floors can exceed 12 feet.

The code also requires that all treads and risers be of uniform width in any one story.

Local codes may vary in some particulars and may place some special restrictions. It is always wise to check with a building inspector.

Light steel *stringers, widely spaced steel balusters form delicate-appearing stair. Treads are polished mahogany. Lake visible through window. Alan Liddle, architect.*

Stairway *connects both levels of hillside home to two-story combination terrace-garden-living room. Designer Rodney Walker made the stair a dramatically cantilevered one.*

Conventional *stringers and treads join forces with iron railing and a view window to make a breathtakingly open flight of stairs. Henry Hill was the architect.*

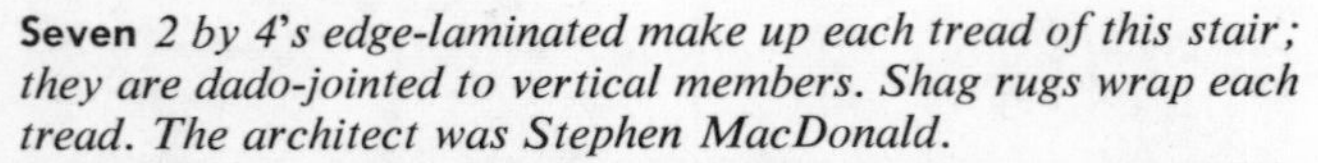

Seven *2 by 4's edge-laminated make up each tread of this stair; they are dado-jointed to vertical members. Shag rugs wrap each tread. The architect was Stephen MacDonald.*

Waxed oak *balustrade is made of a heavy railing and 1⅛-inch balusters. Railing is thicker at top than bottom for appearance, grip. The architect was Ralph D. Anderson.*

Carved balusters *still find a place in many homes. This set marks the edge of a cozy library, in handy reach of a cozy fire. Clifford McBride was the designer.*

Small windows *make spiral bright, cheery. House design was by Al Levy.*

Spiral *staircase leads to adult retreat in this home by architect Mario Corbett.*

Dramatic *stairs swirl twice around two columns. Architects: Hyum & Whitney.*

Underplayed *drama: The spiral stairs hide behind screen. Architect Edward J. LaBelle used ceiling-hung outer rods.*

Spiral stairs

Spiral stairs can hardly be governed by the considerations expressed to this point. Yet they have a lingering appeal, and some practical benefits to bestow upon their owners. They take about a quarter of the space required by conventional stairs, they are self-supporting on their own center columns, and they have an open, airy grace that is most difficult to achieve in an ordinary staircase.

Almost every city has building code provisions dealing specifically with spiral stairs in dwellings. Few or no codes prohibit them providing they comply with general restrictions on width of run (horizontal distance between risers), and height of riser. These standards are imposed to ensure safe footing and head clearance. But inspectors may rule out spiral stairs on individual case conditions. Usually, the reasons are that the stairs are potentially dangerous because of the condition of the structure itself or because of hazards posed by locating them in certain places in a house. Spiral stairs used only by adults, and never in emergency, can sometimes crowd code provisions.

Always see the building inspector before you start; it is the one sure way to avoid expensive back-tracking.

Spiral stairs can be made of either wood or metal. Most are of metal. The metal types are prefabricated and preassembled in a plant (see in the telephone directory of any large city under: Stair builders, Iron Ornamental Work, or Ornamental Iron Work). After the fit is assured, the stairs are knocked down for delivery. Match-marks on each piece make reassembly quick and inexpensive.

Costs range widely, but for a staircase 5 feet in diameter, 9½ feet high, with 12 treads and 13 risers, center column, railing, platform, and prime paint, an average price would approach $600, delivered in the city of manufacture. Trucking costs to distant points are not large. The staircase noted above can be shipped 200 miles for about $25.

Few firms will design staircases; they prefer to leave that department to professionals. But they will make a design fit if they are given the precise dimensions required (floor to finished floor, diameter of opening). Most firms like to have snapshots of the area where the proposed stairs will fit.

Homeowners have a choice of right or left hand stairs. The right hand stair spirals so the railing is on the right side as you go up. Vice versa for left hand.

Saving steps... it pays when the lot slopes

Gravity may seem to be an implacable foe to many hillside dwellers, but it often can be bent to the will of an imaginative designer.

A family fortunate enough to have some control over the design of a new house can often find ways to build in chutes, slides, or incline elevators that do away with a good part of up-and-down carrying of supplies.

For example, the basement trapdoor shown below suggests a reverse of the same idea where the carport is lower than the floor of a house. A door high in the adjoining wall of the carport might lead to the back of a kitchen cabinet. Arriving groceries placed in the cabinet from the carport can be retrieved from the kitchen side after an empty-handed trip up the stairs.

Let there be fair warning: That mail box chute attracts practical jokers, who have used it to deliver a hurricane lamp (it arrived intact and is now a part of the decor), eggs (which arrived less than whole and needed discarding), and a cannonball. A mail box affixed to a pulley clothesline can be reeled in and out.

One great boon for two-story homes is the built-in central vacuum cleaner. The power unit is located in a basement or garage; baseboard outlets (they look much like electric outlets) serve each room. Hoses as long as 26 feet cover areas up to 700 square feet, and the hose is all the housekeeper has to carry. Costs run from $250 to $700.

Near sea, *salt collected on high windows rapidly. Perforated pipe now washes glass automatically.*

Five pairs *of doors at grade level are easy way to put gear in basement in house by architect Marshall W. Perrow.*

In two-story *home, cleaning equipment is closeted at mid-flight of stairs. Architect was Halsey Jones.*

Three-part *chute to basement laundry sorts clothes, stores them just above washer. Architect: John Stafford.*

Chute *from mail box is section of standard pre-fabricated 12-inch heating duct. Hole cut in bottom of box.*

Trash chute *is of heavy galvanized steel 20 by 14 inches. Not used for garbage. J. A. Gooch design.*

Landscaping

Sometimes sloping landscapes distress their owners because they present several equally good ways to develop handsome gardens.

It is a happy kind of trouble to have. The choice between a planted bank and a rugged stone wall may exist here while elsewhere it is a matter of designing a raised planting bed to get some prized plants into close viewing range. At still another place in the garden there is a golden opportunity to devise a set of striking steps.

The stories connected with the photos are to be found as follows: top photo, page 82; next photo, page 77; third photo, page 84; and bottom photo, page 103.

On a view site, the terrace can go in a sheltered nook alongside the house, on a high corner of the lot, or right at the crest of the slope, as close to the view as you can get it.

There is a practical side to developing a hillside site, too. Driveways, car parking, service yards, play space for the children, and such matters take up room.

Plans for hillside sites should be developed with great care. Seemingly innocent grading, paving, or watering can trigger astonishingly serious results if undertaken without thought. But proper planning can avert almost any such troubles. Persons planning to do much of their own landscaping from bare ground up should also read the succeeding chapters on gardening and on home-buying.

	natural slopes	graded slopes
Shallow slope **If graded,** *low bank offers little difficulty. Plant or use low wall. On natural slope, house foundation will be exposed on one side. Consider creating a two-level terraced garden on down slope, with upper level even with house floor level. Use low wall between garden levels; connect with path, ramp, or steps.*	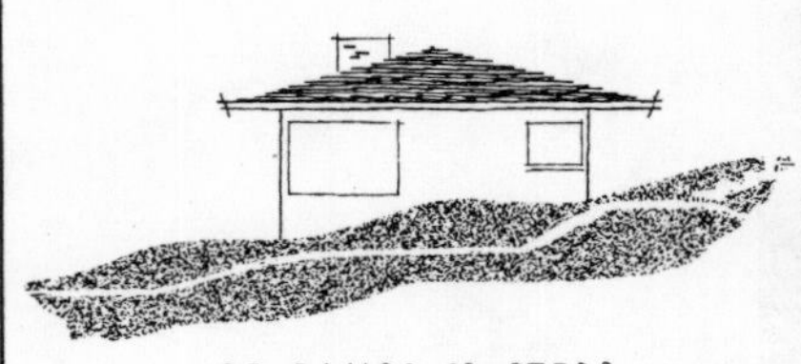 	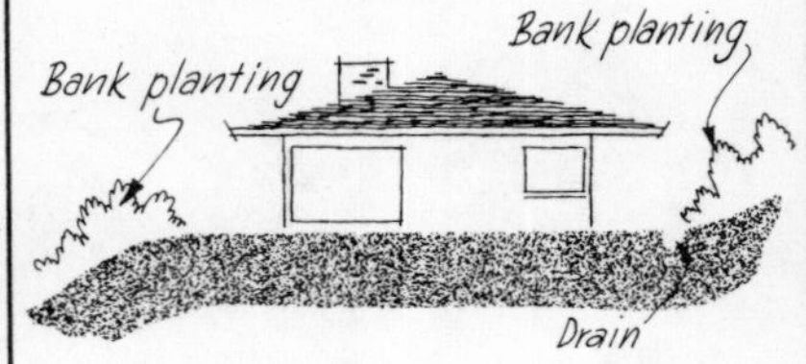
Medium slope **On graded** *site, bank control is biggest problem. On natural site, split level house is one answer—you step out directly to garden from each level. Problem is where to establish level patio area. Medium slopes offer interesting gardens without serious problems of steep slopes. You may want to use plants to screen roofs below.*	 	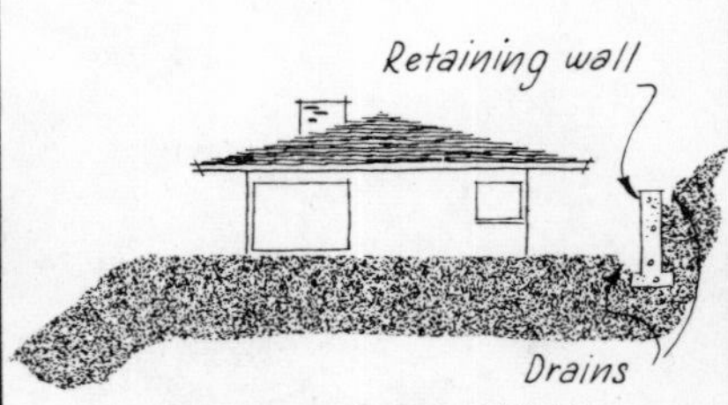
Steep slope **On graded** *site watch the banks. When wet, filled earth may slip and slide down. Cut banks, although usually more stable, also can erode, slide. If in doubt, consult engineer. On natural site, only patio possible may be a deck. Plant a garden to look down on. Space under deck is often useful as a lathhouse, garden work area.*	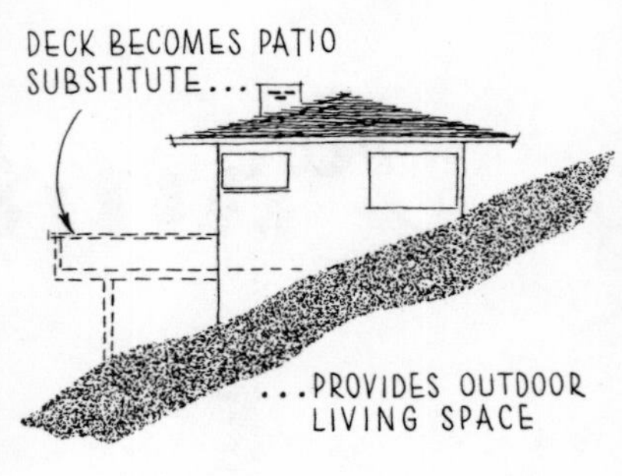 	

There are sites that slope in two directions, sites that follow the natural contour of the terrain, sites that have been cut out with a bulldozer, steep sites, and shallow ones.

If there is one lesson to be learned from their variety, it is that hillside lots can differ radically, even in a subdivision where they were all graded at the same time. Some of them can be real mavericks, suggesting no immediate or simple landscape plan.

Your hillside may have some points in common with the ones shown in sketches or photographs, but no two sites are ever the same. Instead of looking for a plan to copy, look rather for planning principles—the way land has been terraced, the way decks float out over steep drops, the way houses are set to provide sheltered pockets for patios or play yards.

Success in handling a hillside landscaping problem comes most easily to those who consider (but do not always follow) these simple principles:

- Never allow a slope to remain devoid of stabilizing plants, contours, or other retaining devices through a winter whether you are landscaping a lot for the first time or are remodeling an old garden. (This is one simple principle that should always be followed; the others can be taken more lightly).
- Use a series of low retaining walls rather than one high one.
- Use the raised planting bed idea to take care of a slight change of level. Wide terraces on a slope permit a great variety in types of planting.
- Curved banks where the possibility exists may enhance the interest in a garden.
- Utilize plants that prefer hillsides (there are several helpful lists later in this chapter). Generally, you can get a beautiful garden more quickly on a sloping lot than on a level piece of land.

streetside slopes

Street above

Your entry garden *may be partially private, may be sheltered from wind by bank and house. If space is adequate, you may want a front patio. Bank planting can be garden display to enjoy from inside house.*

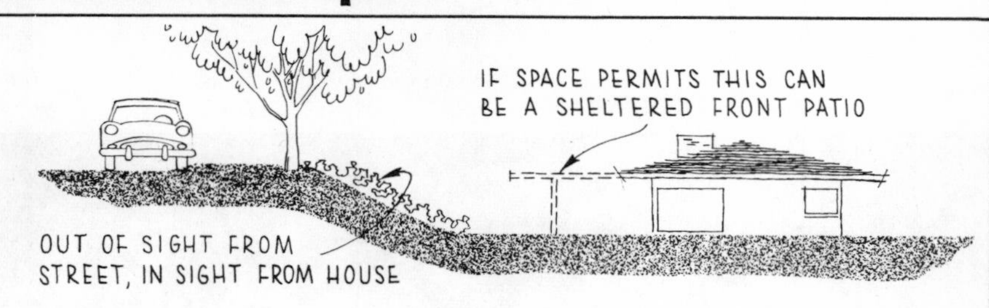

Street below

Your entry garden *may be in public view. You must carry packages up. If grade is steep, use ramps, landings to ease the climb. Try to make steps generous, individual flights short. Try for neat, low maintenance planting.*

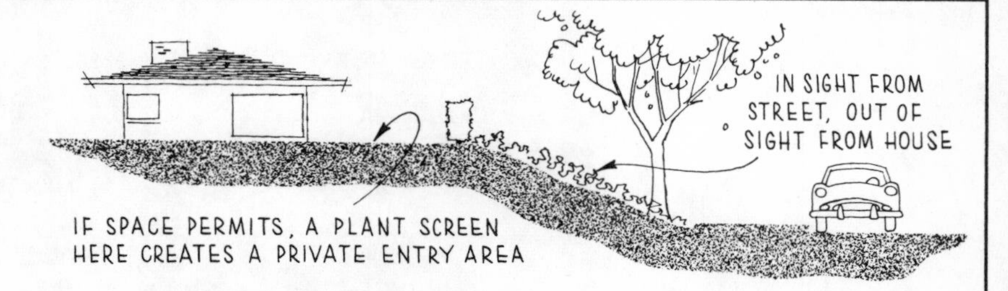

back garden slopes

Bank in view

Either blot out *the bank or make it a pleasant backdrop for your garden. Consider a raised bed or a seat wall at the base of the bank, occasional trees at base, vines stretched on wires, or ground covers grown directly on the bank.*

Bank out of view

You will want *to plant out the bank as a courtesy to neighbors and for erosion control. Consider seat wall at edge of bank; trees or shrubs in bank, with the tops in view above the edge. Trellis of vines can extend illusion of flat space.*

• Consider wood decks in place of terraces wherever you want a level spot. They interfere with soil stability less.

• Shallow risers and wide treads make the most inviting garden steps.

• Steep banks can be hidden by trees planted at their bases, or by private gardens surrounded by screens. But steep banks can also be natural plant display stages.

• The following 45 pages elaborate on all of the challenges mentioned here, and add some new ones. The photographs and sketches represent outstanding solutions to hillside landscape problems.

sideyard slopes

Can he see *into your windows? One answer is trees on property line—or cooperative planting. If sideyard is narrow, a fence saves space. On a slight slope, a low retaining wall will eliminate the bank, save more space. Can you see into his windows? Cooperative fencing or planting is a good answer. If you have a wide sideyard, a combination fence and lath shelter will put the area to good use.*

The happy problem...how to handle a view

Bigleaf *maples form a leafy frame and a sunshade for view of Aurora Bridge in Seattle. Architect Harrison Overturf can expand view with pruning shears.*

Sword-leafed *plants, palms break up expansive ocean view with bold, sculptured leaves. The landscape architect was Fred Lang.*

Perhaps it seems inconceivable that you could improve a spectacular, unobstructed panorama that offers a patchwork of colors and shapes by day, and a sparkling collection of jewels by night. But often it can be done. Perhaps it seems inconceivable that you could retrieve a view from a sea of rooftops. But often it can be done. Here, we suggest some approaches to a view site.

The full view

You might call this the ultimate: A site that fulfills the dream to be perched high on a hilltop or ocean cliff, with the best nature can provide spread at your feet, and the effect of man's harsher contributions softened by distance.

A question which provokes differing opinions from landscape architects and architects (and homeowners) is: Should unobstructed views be altered or not? Some contend that a panoramic view, like a rich meal, can satiate so that you lose interest; that sweeping views should be broken up by trees so the scene in effect is "edited," more provocative, easier to absorb.

Others prefer a view that is undiluted, one that hits you with all its force. What if you do begin to take the view for granted? It becomes an important and enriching part of your life, and you do not have to be consciously aware of it all the time to enjoy it.

Perhaps, in the long run, the best position is somewhere in the middle. But if you feel strongly either way, and if you work with an architect or landscape architect, be sure to make your position clear to him from the start.

There is one problem inherent in many view sites, especially in the West. Very often they face the setting sun, and from midafternoon until sunset you have to pull the shades and forget the view. Wherever the view is toward the setting sun even proponents of the uncluttered, unedited view are likely to acknowledge soon the need for an eyebrow of foliage from a vine trained on a trellis across a window, or over a deck or patio—or possibly a row of trees whose branches are trimmed above the window level, so that you look through the branches and between the trunks to the view

Pines hide *neighboring house, invite viewers to look out across lagoon. Landscape architect: Douglas Baylis.*

Part open *screen focuses on un-built hills, hides clusters of houses. Landscape architects: Armstrong & Sharfman.*

Ironwood tree (*Casuarina equistefolia*) *frames west-facing view across a small bay, and is good sun-shade.*

Deck edits *a swarm of houses out of ocean view for viewers from this window. Architect: Philip Fisk.*

(which may strike you as even more exciting than it was before).

If you have purchased a lot and plan to build, give the site some careful thought before you locate the house on the spot with the best view. You may decide to reserve that spot for the garden terrace, arbor, deck, or garden house so you will be forced out of the house to enjoy the finest vantage point.

Some designers we talked with like a garden area as subdued as the view is exciting. Instead of stunning you with the view as you go up the entry walk, they would rather bring you first into a simple entry court, saving the best until you enter the living room or walk out onto a deck. And sometimes they suggest a dining room or study that simply turns its back on the view and looks out instead on a small enclosed garden which is a frank respite from the awesome scope of things on the other side of the house.

The partial view

Gardens in this group far outnumber those with full, spectacular views. More than likely you will have to look between houses or over rooftops for your view.

Views of this kind need editing to blot out objects you don't want to see —a neighbor's house, a busy road, a parking or service area, antennae, or power poles.

Sometimes a screen six to eight feet long will be all you need. In other situations you may have to combine planting and structure (screen or arbor) into a more elaborate device before you do much enhancing of the view.

In some cases a potential view goes unnoticed. The problem may be that your eye sees too much. If there is no outstanding subject to narrow your attention you do not focus closely on anything in particular. One of the best ways to sort out the possibilities is to study the whole scene through the lens or viewfinder of a camera. That is, pan the entire garden and everything beyond it —distant hills, the trees on the skyline, vistas between rooftops. This exercise will focus your eye on a series of cropped views.

Or go a step further and take photographs of the most promising scenes, then crop with bits of paper to eliminate eyesores or play up points of interest. This will suggest where to put screens or planting.

Think twice before you design your entire garden around a view, however. It may be the most exciting thing in the world when you first move in; but how you intend to *live* in the garden is all important.

Almost every designer will agree that the view should be treated as only one element of the site, and that it should be utilized in the way it best fits with all your objectives for the site.

In just five years...raw cut to beautiful bank

First step: *Laying drain lines. Then air drill bored planting holes along face of bank. In foreground fill, holes dug by hand and filled with humus.*

Early plantings *take shape. Tall, thick growing shrubs and trees along lower portion of bank make it appear less steep than it actually is.*

The earth scar in the photo directly to the left is what the owners of this site saw from the windows of their house when they first moved in. It was hard to believe that anything would ever grow enough to cover that steep, rocky bank.

Yet, as the photo on the facing page demonstrates, they used plants successfully to erase the scar. The photo at lower left shows how things stood 13 months after the bank was first planted.

This is an especially tough situation, the cut bank that has been scraped to bare rock, and one that should give hope to the owners of the least promising of natural banks.

Here is how this determined couple attacked the problem (with the help of a landscape architect), and how they have maintained the bank to provide a healthy environment.

The first task was to install five sumps and drain lines, to handle the water problem. You can see one location in the photo of the raw bank. To shield the bank from water from the lot above, there is a 12-inch high berm at the property line. Along with these precautions against water went a complex automatic sprinkling system.

Then planting got under way. The landscape crew, working on ladders for secure footing, bored holes in the bank with an air drill. The holes were made larger than usual and filled with good soil to get the shrubs, trees, and ground covers off to the best possible start. The planting mix was half leaf mold, half garden loam, and with a handful of bonemeal mixed in for each hole.

After all plants were in and well watered, a 1-inch mulch of pine shavings was spread over all exposed soil and in plant basins. Each two weeks the owners applied a light hand feeding of nitrogen fertilizer. Each month a small handful of bloodmeal was applied to each plant basin. Faithful watering and weeding resulted in the plants' rapid growth through their first year.

From that point forward, maintenance has not been unusually difficult, but now that plants are large a comprehensive program of pruning is essential. Watering and once-a-year fertilizing are necessary to keep plants in lush condition. Ammonium sulfate is broadcast over the bank at the rate of one pound per 100 square feet during the late spring months. Since most of the plants

What was *once a steep unfriendly bank is now hidden. Slow starters have taken over from the fast growing plants that served at first to cover the bare ground and prevent erosion. Watering and pruning have become the main maintenance tasks.*

are relatively pest-free, the owners have no spray program. Weeds have not encroached greatly because ice plant, Algerian ivy, honeysuckle and sweet alyssum cover the bank areas.

Watering continues to be a problem as plants grow larger. Rotating sprinklers must run for longer periods to get adequate coverage. Some areas require canvas soakers to get water to spots where plants obstruct the sprinkler pattern. The sprinkler heads are also raised to accommodate the increased height.

The choice of plants in this garden was keyed to the crucial need for erosion control. Fast growing plants such as ice plant, *Solanum rantonnetii*, Pampas grass, cassia, white rockrose, and *Echium fastuosum* did the initial job of covering the bare ground while slower starters such as purple hop bush, bottlebrush, xylosma, and star jasmine were getting established.

Trees provide the most permanent erosion control and increase privacy. Best performers have been the following: orchid tree (*Bauhinia variegata*), now 15 feet high; Modesto ash, 20 feet high; and eucalyptus trees in variety.

Plants *at 13-month stage. Fast growers and slow growers give garden a permanent framework. Shrubs, trees and billowing ground covers begin to blend.*

Low-growing *ground covers on a slope can be used to achieve a lawn-like effect, or can be chosen for color, as in this case. Landscape architects Thompson and Thompson chose daylily for its heavy summer bloom.*

Different effect *than that above was obtained through use of shrubby asparagus fern backed with bushman's poison, fern pine. Landscape architect: Warren Jones.*

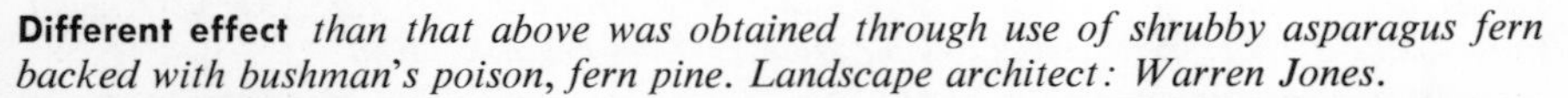

Fast-growing *Cotoneaster 'Lofast' trails gracefully down steep bank. It shows red berries in fall.*

Yellow trailing *gazania is the ground cover here. Designer: Mildred Davis.*

Flat stones, *Vinca minor control this slope against both water runoff and wind erosion. Utah oak, sagebrush.*

Hiding a bank from view

Rocky slope *rises just to left of walk. Grid screen of 2 by 2's hides the bank, focusses attention on a tiny close-up garden. Landscape architect: William Kapranos.*

Trees *at foot hide this rocky slope. Landscape architect Zareh Kiragh prepared special planting pockets behind brick wall so eucalyptus could acclimate to soil.*

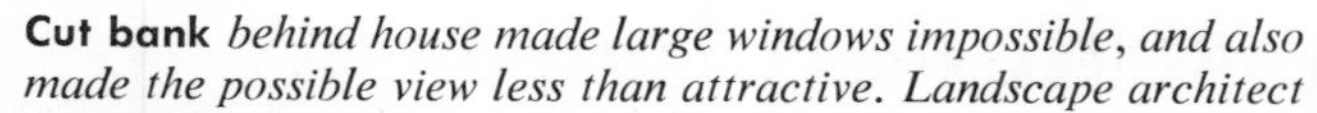

Cut bank *behind house made large windows impossible, and also made the possible view less than attractive. Landscape architect*

L.K. Smith solved privacy and view problem with this bathroom garden behind plastic panels.

Stairs *at left of carport lead down through low-maintenance bank planting of heathers,* Ceanothus gloriosus, Vinca minor, *mugho pines and Oregon grape. Steps are made of 2x12 stringers with cast concrete pads centered in gravel beds.*

The retaining walls are softened by plants

LANDSCAPE ARCHITECT: ROBERT W. CHITTOCK

Gravel bank *was cut back to the right and the fill was used to make a flat shelf building site for the three-level house. Double carport, which adjoins kitchen is level with street and is reached by a bridge across the slope.*

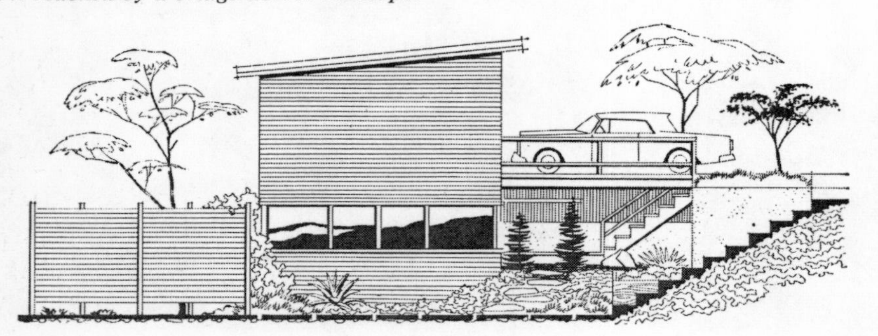

In the opinion of some, a beautiful view justifies tackling the problems of a difficult building site. For this new house, the owners chose a lot high on a bluff overlooking island-dotted Puget Sound, with the Olympic Mountains in the background; at night city lights of both Tacoma and Seattle brighten the sky. Architects A. O. Bumgardner and Partners designed a three-level house well suited to needs of an active couple with two small children.

The landscape problems of such a site soon became apparent.

Plantings were needed to draw attention to the front entrance (down a flight of steps from the street), and to soften 6-foot-high concrete retaining walls. In addition, the owners wanted level play space for the children, privacy from neighbors higher on the hill, and a way to go up and down a

Overhead *trellis, at foot of stairs in photo at left, creates shade for small paved terrace and supports wisteria vine.*

From street *you look down the steps toward entrance which is located to the right of the garage deck. This lower deck is eight inches above ground level and is flanked on either side by tall rhododendrons and low hostas.*

Overhead *is the underside of the carport bridge. Area beneath is gravel, highlighted with evergreens and boulders, for play yard and outdoor storage.*

gravelly bank.

Finally, they wanted the whole garden to be easy to maintain.

The photographs show how landscape architect Robert W. Chittock used both plantings and structures to solve these problems. Evergreen ground covers *Vinca minor* and *Ceanothus gloriosus* thrive on the open slopes. They hold the banks and create the same cool green look of lawn on a level lot.

Since visitors approach the garden from above, there's an added, unusual perspective of the garden. They look down into the flower clusters and foliage of rhododendrons, at the flaring clumps of hosta, and across the top of a trellis covered with wisteria. And they see the pleasant pattern that the concrete stepping stones make down the hillside when viewed from above.

A bridge *leads from the second story, where bedrooms are located in the house, to a secluded uphill sitting area (to the right).*

A series of planting beds holds the slope

LANDSCAPE ARCHITECT: ECKBO, ROYSTON AND WILLIAMS

There was no easy way to approach the landscaping problem this site presented. A steep uphill bank rose almost directly from the back of the house. There was the usual drainage problem to contend with. Space for gardening or outdoor living was meager.

However, as you can see from these photographs, the optimistic owners, guided by landscape architects Eckbo, Royston & Williams, found such a site both a challenge and an opportunity.

Henry Hill, the architect of the house, gave the plan its first fanciful start with a footbridge from the second floor to what later was to become an upper level sun trap. The rest of the garden was planned with a series of interlocking, stoutly constructed walls, raised beds, and steps.

Once engineering problems were solved, plantings were worked out to soften edges and to create a garden that could be enjoyed from above, below, or at eye level.

Steps *traverse hill. Lush juniper and vinca soften concrete planting beds.*

Looking up *to footbridge. Wood walls terrace steep slope.*

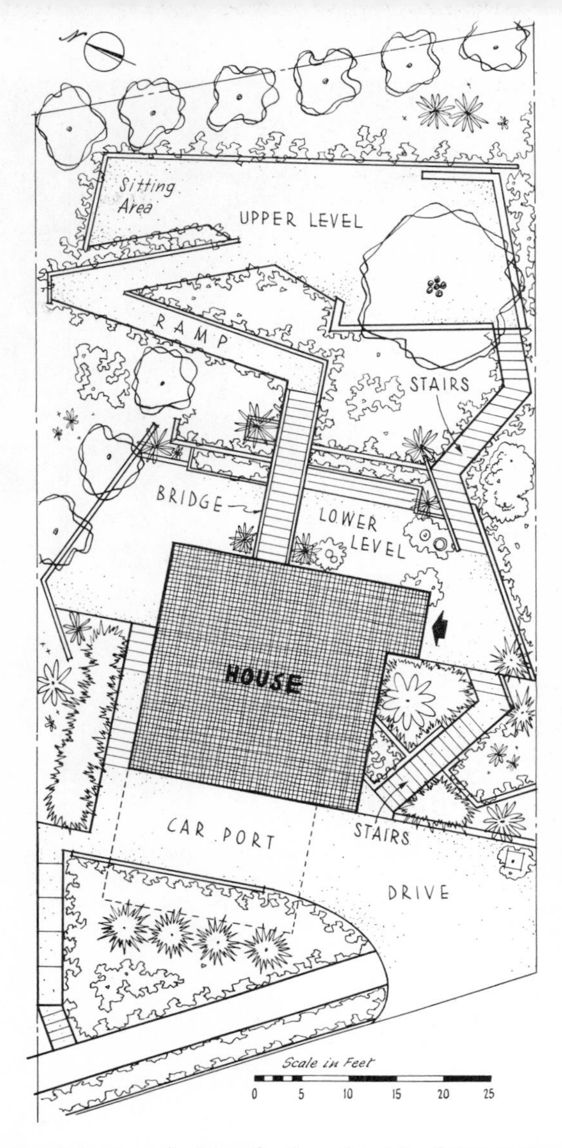

Bank, *terraced to make raised beds, is planted with dwarf azalea, sedum (above seat). Steps lead up the side of the garden.*

Shallow pool *is used at the base of this concrete retaining wall to dress up its appearance and enhance patio setting. Landscape architects: Kitchen & Hunt; fountain by Robert Dhaemers.*

Plastic vaults *and trellis cut off neighbor's view into patio; with help of plantings it hides 12-foot retaining wall from owners' view. Architect was John Hans Ostwald.*

Overhead shelter *makes private garden out of what used to be a narrow trough. Roof benefits azaleas, ivy geranium in raised bed. Design: Solomone & Hoy.*

Walls must be functional, but they don't have to look it

For people who live in the hills or who plan to buy hillside sites, mechanical soil-holding devices are an almost inevitable part of building and landscaping plans.

A few lots can be controlled entirely by means of bank planting, as the garden shown on pages 76-77 suggests, and some parts of every lot lend themselves to that solution. On the other hand, some type of wall will serve most lots well in one place or another.

A raised bed may stop seepage from a higher point. Terracing may be the answer to locating a patio. A retaining wall may make possible what would be otherwise an "impossible" building site. This paragraph points out one extreme and the other in uses of soil-holding walls. Of course there are an infinite number of in-between needs for walls. The main thing to remember in planning a wall is that you are conducting a small war with gravity, and that this is serious business.

Retaining walls in developments

Thousands of present hillside dwellers could increase their usable lot size and add to their level outdoor living area by

Vine *covers trellis to edit view below and hides retaining wall from below. Chief benefit is apparent increase in size of narrow garden. Design: Eckbo, Royston & Williams.*

Plant display *bench doubles as a bank-holding crib. Uprights of the open lath structure are set in concrete piers. Designed by Harold Whitaker to shade orchids, hide bank above.*

Brick terraces *match lines and material of the house. Steps relate to wall and drive. Planting concentrated in corners.*

Flagstone *veneer on concrete wall ties with house. Retaining wall designed to keep mud, rocks off driveway.*

Stone-in-mortar *wall is turned into a utility yard by cantilevered clothesline. Walls reflect heat, aid drying.*

installing retaining walls.

Many shelf lots, now being carved out of steep hillsides by the hundreds, would be far better home sites after some cutting or filling and the installation of a retaining wall.

In many cities the subdivider or builder is limited to a 33° fill slope and a 45° cut slope grade. Within these limits he normally levels a lot of the minimum size allowed by the building codes. Because he must add the cost onto his selling price, he seldom builds retaining walls to increase level area. Buyers can often enlarge and improve such a lot. If the house has not yet been built, it is often possible to arrange with the builder to build walls and do the necessary additional grading before the house is built.

Walls for erosion control

Almost the only sure way to protect some hillsides against soil failure and erosion is the construction of properly engineered retaining walls.

Depending upon the site, a retaining wall may be necessary behind the house, in front of the house, or in both places.

The retaining wall behind the house, coupled with a surface drainage device, helps stabilize the soil on the slope, supporting it when it becomes waterlogged and abnormally heavy. Wall and drain working together perform the function of the "toe" of a normal slope, protecting structures from damage and permitting outdoor living on the upslope side of the structure.

The retaining wall below the house, set on original grade, helps to stabilize the soil under the garden and lawn. By preventing slippage here, you may save an expensive job of repairing cracked or settled patio paving, or an even more expensive job of earth moving and refilling. The below-the-house wall also

A compendium of walls. *At top left, massive granite boulders are stepped back on a bank, a frequently-used device on gentle banks but not good on steep slopes. Top center, two walls are built with two materials. The lower is flagstone laid with mortar; the upper is native stone laid dry. Upper right, bricks laid dry in a curving and inward sloping wall (see sketches); again the slope is very slight. Middle row left, a crib of railroad ties designed by Peggy Sullivan. Center, a crib of peeled poles. These walls will rot away in 15 years or so, and cannot be stacked high. Lower right, a low wall of broken concrete by Ruth Patricia Shellhorn. Each course is true horizontal to minimize down flow of water. Directly left, a crib of 2 by 4's designed by Walter and Florence Gerke (sketch on next page).*

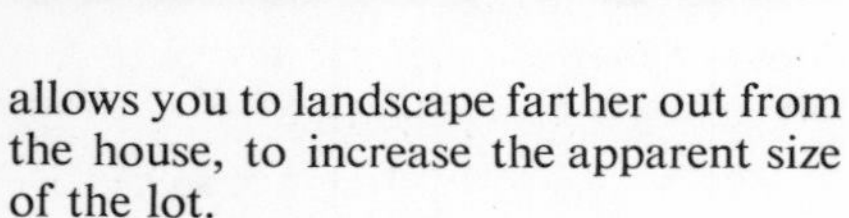

allows you to landscape farther out from the house, to increase the apparent size of the lot.

Reclaiming impossible sites

You have probably driven past many unoccupied stretches of steep land on which you could never visualize a house. Many such lots are totally unsuitable. Some of them, however, can become excellent building sites if you install retaining walls and do the proper grading and filling. Sometimes it is possible to take a grim-looking $4,000 lot, spend $3,000 in grading and filling, and come out with a lot that is worth $10,000 or more.

Big developers do such land "improvement" on a big scale. Small builders are continually looking for these sleeper hillside lots for individual speculation. If you look carefully, you may be able to spot one on your own.

Grading hillside sites

The cost of cutting and filling is hard to estimate. Not only do the mechanical steps differ from one site to another, there is the question of how the cut or fill is done. You will face one of these general situations: Direct cut and fill, cut and export, or import and fill.

Cut and fill. Generally speaking, this is the least expensive. The cut-away earth is used as fill right on the site. If you can plan the cubic yardage of your cut to equal the required fill, the material generally can be bulldozed or skip-loaded from one area to the other. For this type of job, measure the length of the cut or fill; multiply by the average width of the cut, then multiply again by the average height of the cut—all in yards.

Earth-moving contractors caution that costs may vary widely depending upon the kind of soil, the contours of the site, and how much the contractor must protect the existing landscape (see page 116).

Cut and export. In many urban areas, this is the most expensive choice. If you must haul excess soil to a dumping ground, you may have to pay from $2 to as much as $10 per cubic yard, depending upon topography and the distance the mover must transport the unwanted soil. If you can find a lot owner

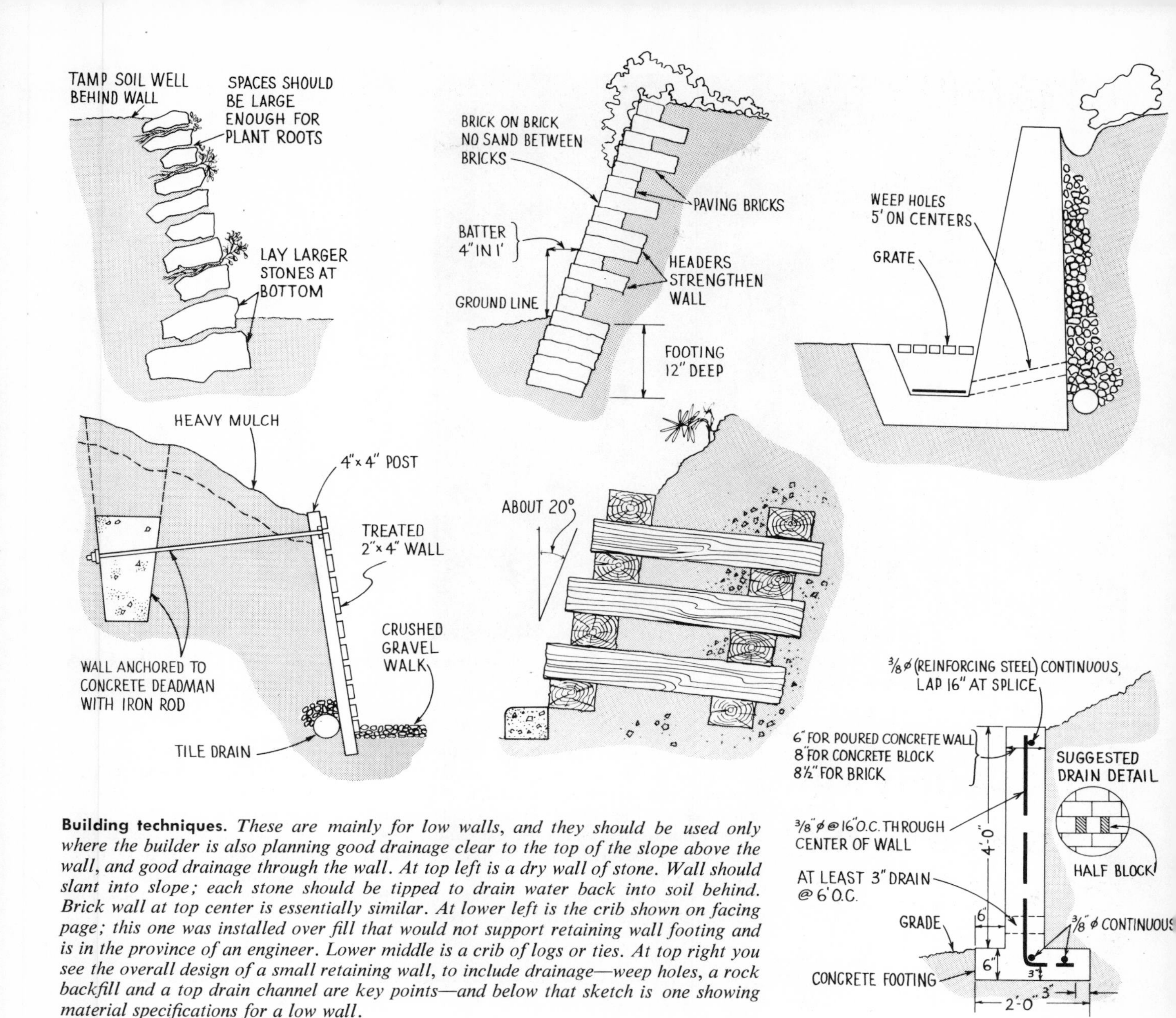

Building techniques. *These are mainly for low walls, and they should be used only where the builder is also planning good drainage clear to the top of the slope above the wall, and good drainage through the wall. At top left is a dry wall of stone. Wall should slant into slope; each stone should be tipped to drain water back into soil behind. Brick wall at top center is essentially similar. At lower left is the crib shown on facing page; this one was installed over fill that would not support retaining wall footing and is in the province of an engineer. Lower middle is a crib of logs or ties. At top right you see the overall design of a small retaining wall, to include drainage—weep holes, a rock backfill and a top drain channel are key points—and below that sketch is one showing material specifications for a low wall.*

nearby who needs soil, try to sign him up for your "gift." It will save money by shortening the distance the soil needs to be exported. It is a good idea to get a written statement from the site owner saying that he authorizes the dumping. If compaction of fill is required, be sure that it will cost less than transporting the soil to some more distant point.

Import and fill. This type of job is often the least expensive. Every now and then you can get fill virtually free-of-charge. In some areas, earth-movers not only will provide free fill but will often compact it and supply free soil tests to avoid long-distance hauls. The market for dirt fluctuates wildly with supply and demand. To check on this market, talk with various contractors or with your local municipal building department.

Building a retaining wall

Whether or not you can build a retaining (or other) wall depends first of all on the scope of the project. Secondarily, it depends upon your masonry skill and the amount of time you can put in.

A wall of four feet or more often calls for professional work, and in many cases must be designed by a licensed engineer. Up to that point, many homeowners will do their own work after having their plans checked out by a building inspector.

Amateurs should never attempt to solve their own design problems if the slope they are working with has any tendency to slip, or if there is to be considerable fill behind the proposed wall.

Always check with a building department before launching a project. You will find out if permits are required, and you will get good advice whether or not a permit is involved.

The accompanying sketch describes adequate reinforcement for masonry walls to four feet. Low walls and raised beds can also be fashioned from stone laid dry or in mortar or some kind of cribbing (wood or pre-cast concrete).

Cribbing, which is generally used on fill ground too unstable to accommodate the footing of a retaining wall, should be designed and built by a professional. The sketch shows the basic principle.

Looking down *from above, the strong modular pattern of the retaining wall emerges from the sharp drop in the concrete walk to the poolside terrace below.*

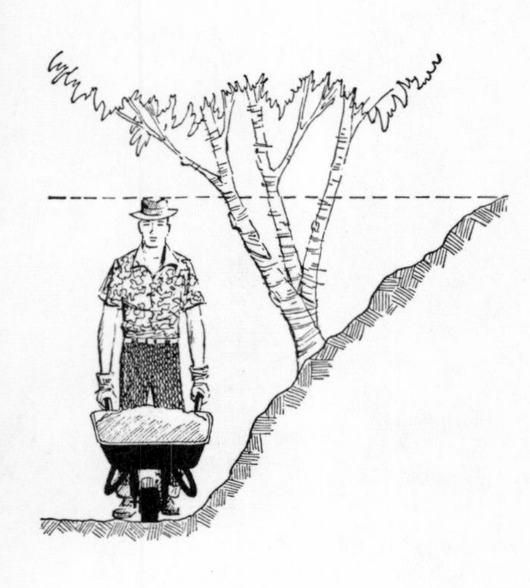

The problem: *A steep, 6-foot bank with no level planting area available.*

Garden for a steep bank

LANDSCAPE ARCHITECT:
ECKBO, ROYSTON AND WILLIAMS

Gardeners who live on a steep hillside establish a garden in one of two ways: They plant a raw bank with shrubs, trees, and vines, cutting pockets into the side of the bank for the plants; or they find some way to convert the bank into level planting areas.

The sketch illustrates the particular problem that faced architect Henry Hill in his Berkeley garden. Below, we show you how landscape architects Eckbo, Royston & Williams solved it with a series of modular retaining walls. These provide the level planting spaces that make gardening easier. Because these walls have strong architectural lines, they also tie the bank to the house and to the surrounding terraces.

Retaining wall *at base of hill doubles as bench. Facing matches house siding.*

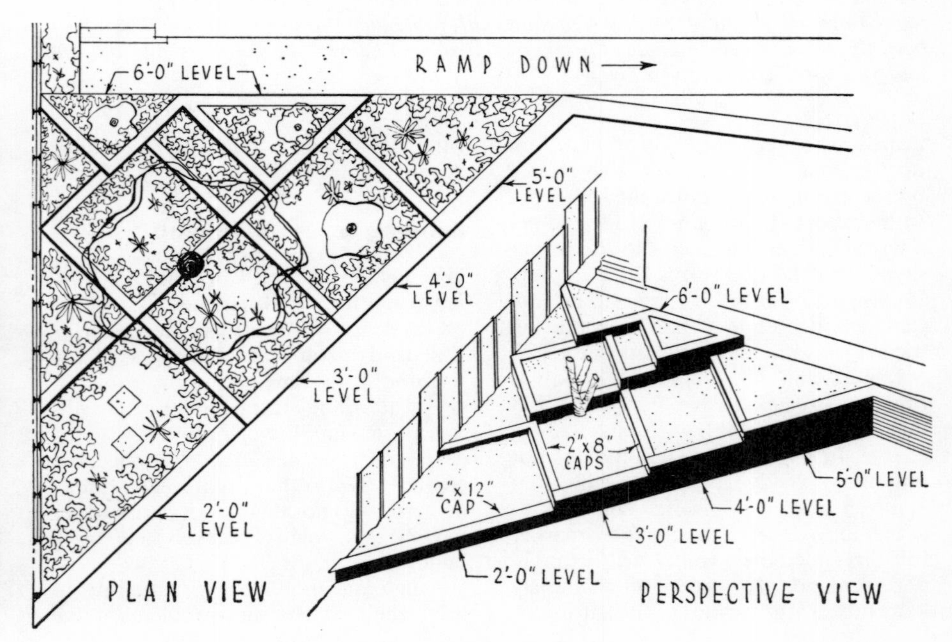

Transformed *garage roof. Landscape architects built a garden onto the roof with portable plant boxes and deck sections. Mexican pebbles add to the "garden" space without weight of soil. All plants are chosen for shallow rooting habits.*

Garden for a rooftop deck

LANDSCAPE ARCHITECT: ARMSTRONG & SHARFMAN

Installing a garden on a roof is usually more complicated than putting one on a deck originally designed to support weight. In this example, the problem was two-fold: How to avoid heavy structural changes, and also how to provide for convenient clearance of the area in case roof repair should become necessary.

It was also desirable to preserve the views to the north and east, and screen out the houses to the west, but not obstruct the westerly afternoon breezes.

Here you see the solution that the owners worked out with landscape architects Armstrong and Sharfman—a completely demountable garden. A series of 4-foot-square modules, some in charcoal-stained decking, others filled with pebbles, form an attractive patterned floor. Storage cabinets and planting boxes can also be lifted out of place.

Dish gardens and tubbed plants decorate the garden with portable color. Planting boxes provide for larger-growing plants.

The raised planters have small openings for drainage; excess water runs off the sloping roof below.

Plan shows *how designers divided rooftop into sitting area and garden. Lightweight overhead serves to focus the view. The cabinets are used to store brazier, folding chairs, and other patio furnishings. They are display shelves, too.*

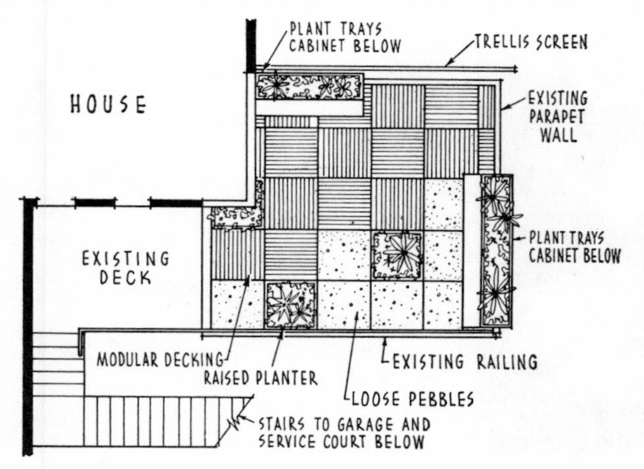

...Rooftops

On a sturdy roof. *Landscape architect Thomas Church divided space with a bamboo screen to make private area off bedroom, and a generous patio for entertaining. The floor is brick. Australian tree fern at right.*

People who enjoy fingers-in-the-dirt gardening as a hobby sometimes find themselves torn between a precipitous site and their enthusiasm for plants. A highly satisfactory compromise for most of them is that of covering the bank with coyote brush or juniper, and building an elaborate container garden on a deck or rooftop.

Deck gardening is also a boon to

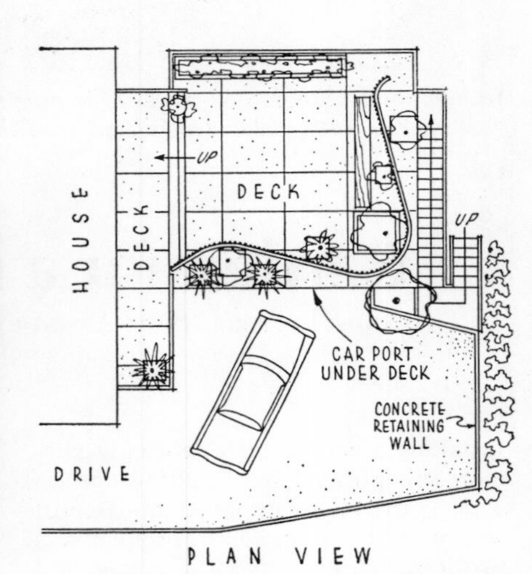

Ignoring a view *that can be enjoyed from other parts of the house, this rooftop garden is the solution to a need for privacy on the downslope side of the house. Landscape architects Eckbo, Royston & Williams designed the garden.*

Low walls *instead of tall fences as above, mark this garden. Both gardens enjoy perimeter planting beds, but this one is worked out so owner can enjoy hobby of growing succulents, and a city skyline. Thomas Church design is modified here.*

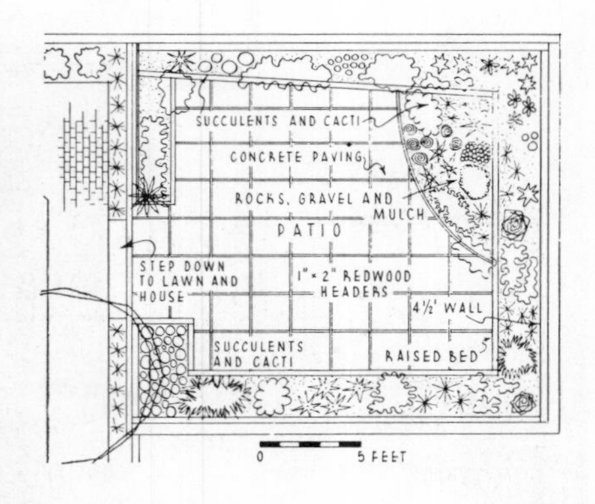

...and decks—special challenges to hillside landscapers

hillside houses with a need for sun or wind control outside the main living areas. Plants in containers are more flexible and often more attractive than screens or roofs as climate control devices.

The story two pages preceeding is one successful response to both needs. The next three pages offer further ideas and techniques for landscaping a deck. (If containers are new to you, the *Sunset* book *Gardening in Containers* can be an invaluable aid in technical gardening matters.)

On a deck, all plants are in containers or in container-like planting beds set at or below the surface. The space is limited, often in full view of the house (and exposed to neighbors). You want the area to look and live like a garden, but with the neatness and comfort of a room. How to avoid stains on the floor? What to do with plants that get too big, or those that look well only part of the year? How to hide the mess of planting and repotting? How to choose plants for sun or wind control? For privacy? And how to make a tiny deck look spacious, or a large deck look snug and inviting?

Recessed planters *provide shade against sun, satisfy owners' wish to grow ornamental plants. Planters rest on deck beams.*

Secluded *garden house is 25 feet above ground, on a deck given over to container plants. Architect: Germano Milono.*

Overhang *protects camellia blooms; lattice work suspension device for hanging baskets. Architect: James E. Hussey.*

Deck extends *patio instead of house. Loquats at grade level break open expanse. Design: Royston, Hanamoto & Mayes.*

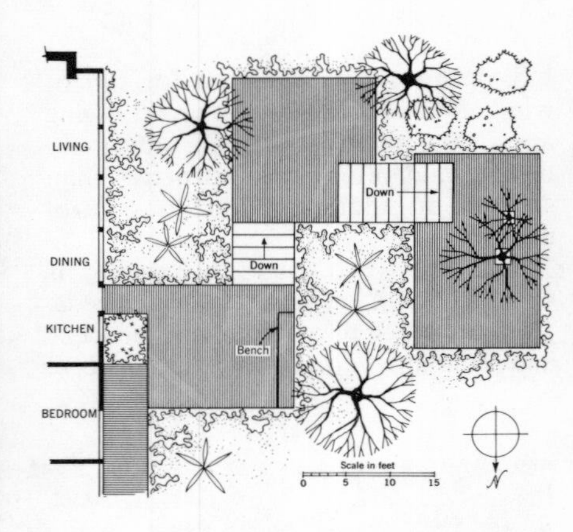

From highest *of three decks, looking down to lowest. Instead of planting on the deck, landscape architect William Teufel made a series of small decks that go down in close contact with the slope and its varied plantings.*

More about landscaping decks

If the deck is small. Make use of upward space with hangers on the walls for ivy or other trailing evergreens, and with swing-out metal arm brackets for hanging baskets of sun-loving annuals. In tubs, use shrubs or small trees that naturally grow tall and narrow. Columnar evergreens such as fir and some pines are especially adapted to this purpose. A row of them can be grouped in tubs for sun control and as a background for flowers in pots.

If the deck is hot. Green foliage can modify climate. Choose plants that can take sun and reflected heat: Persimmons, loquats, pittosporums—even a fig tree should thrive. Water them often in warm weather. For shade, choose a tree that will grow eight or ten feet tall and will spread about as much. If a tree will not do, let a fast-growing annual vine climb to the roof overhang, or cover a trellis.

Soil plus water equals mud. When working with soil, spread out a large plastic dropcloth on the deck. An old card table, perhaps with the legs cut down, makes a fine temporary potting bench. A place to store all gardening paraphernalia is a necessity. An elaborate approach might be a double door closet with a translucent plastic roof to admit light, a sink for washing pots and filling the watering can, storage bins for soil and peat, and storage space for deck furniture. A far less costly approach might be an enclosed space under a bench used to store pots, watering can, and other light equipment.

- If your deck is four feet or more off the ground, rig a rope pulley instead of carrying soil, plants, and containers up steps.
- Use bamboo or regular pipe to extend drain holes of large containers beyond the edges of the deck where a gutter can be used if straight-down drainage would land somewhere you don't want it.
- Keep a hose handy but out of sight. A bib might be rigged in a well with a lift-up trapdoor, or one might be hidden in a storage unit if there is an easy way to rig a faucet on the deck. Otherwise, run the hose up from below and fasten it to the back of a bench or storage cabinet; fix it with a turn-off nozzle so you don't have to go below to turn on and off. Convenient water often spells the difference between adequate and so-so watering.
- Don't overlook the possibility of castors on containers or trays. Castors require tight spacing of deck boards or they are more nuisance than help.

Hose bib *recessed in floor of deck serves several large planters.*

Under *potting bench, hose bib and storage for chairs, barbecue.*

A list of plants for hillside situations

Almost any plant will grow on a slope if given reasonable care. The following lists are, therefore, far from encyclopedic. Rather, they contain the names of plants with proven ability to control erosion, or to endure poor soils and drought, or to grow well on retaining walls or other soil-holding devices. Some of the lists are results of tests by official agencies (these are credited); others are the recommendations of veteran hillside landscapers.

Cultural or botanical information on these plants is not presented systematically here. For such information, there are three Sunset books of great value. These are: *The Sunset Western Garden Book*, *Lawns and Ground Covers*, and *How to Plan, Establish, and Maintain Rock Gardens*. The last named is by George Schenk.

Plants for erosion control

This list is drawn from reports by the United States Forest Service, and the Division of Forestry, State of California

Calocedrus decurrens (incense cedar). The growth of this large, erect coniferous tree may be slow at first, but once established, it may add two feet per year to its height. Dense, narrow crown. Use it in deep soils on shaded slopes. For large areas only.

Heteromeles arbutifolia (Christmas berry). The familiar toyon or Christmas berry is suitable for planting in all deep soils, or in semi-shaded shallow soils. It is extremely attractive, with clusters of bright red berries from November through February, dainty clustered flowers in summer, and stiff green leaves all year. It grows rapidly, reaching 10 to 25 feet.

Prunus ilicifolia (hollyleaf cherry). This attractive plant has glossy, holly-like light green leaves and clusters of small, feathery white flowers from March to May. Handsome in a background or screen planting, or clipped as a hedge. Also is desirable for road slopes in the country, but is badly mutilated by deer. It grows 20 feet high, 8 to 12 feet wide. Shallow soils or competition with faster growing plants slow its growth.

Quercus agrifolia (California live oak) and

Quercus chrysolepis (canyon live oak). These two oaks are large, spreading, slow growing trees recommended for planting in deep soils in partial shade, or in full sun in eroded areas with deep moisture-holding ability.

Quercus wislizenii var. *frutescens* (dwarf interior live oak). Spreading woody shrub or small tree 3 to 12 feet in height with a dense crown. Use it in deep soils in full sun or partial shade. It is rather difficult to establish in shallow soils, but easier if the site is shaded.

Rhus integrifolia (lemonade berry). A compact, evergreen shrub 4 to 9 feet high, depending on site. It has large, roundish, glossy leaves, and clusters of small pink flowers followed by large red berries. An adaptable plant that grows almost anywhere except in very acid soils. Can take temperatures from the hottest down to 20 degrees.

Rhus ovata (sugar bush). This plant has the same characteristics as the lemonade berry except that blooms are creamy white instead of pink. Excellent in full sun in deep and shallow soils. It is frequently used for hedges.

Ceanothus species. Several members of this large plant family of Western natives are effective for erosion control. It is best to use species growing locally. (See further lists below.)

Fremontia californica (flannel bush). A large, woody, strikingly attractive chaparral shrub with wooly-backed leaves and large yellow flowers. Major disadvantage is that it is subject to many diseases. Some say that *Fremontia mexicana* is less so.

Tamarix aphylla (athel). A desert tree used often for windbreaks, athel has a deep and extensive root system and dense crown.

City of Los Angeles list

Cut and fill development in the City of Los Angeles has become extensive enough to require special consideration of plants that will prevent bank erosion. The following plants are approved by the Board of Building and Safety Commissioners (Sec. 91.3007):

"A. Grasses or turf (to be planted at 5 to 10 pounds per 1,000 sq. ft.). The recommended mixture is Purple vetch (½ lb. per 1,000 sq. ft.); Fescue Goar's (5 lbs. per 1,000 sq. ft.); Trefoil (2 lbs. per 1,000 sq. ft.); Approved native plant and wildflower seeds (¼ lb. per 1,000 sq. ft.).

"B. Ground cover plants (in lieu of grasses, to be planted minimum 18 inches on center). 1. *Hedera canariensis* (Algerian ivy); 2. *Ipomoea leari* (Dawn-flower morning glory); 3. *Parthenocissus quinquefolia* (Virginia creeper); 4. *Parthenocissus tricuspidata* (Boston ivy); 5. *Baccharis pilularis* (Dwarf coyote bush); 6. *Hymenocyclus croceus* (*Mesembryanthemum croceum*); 7. *Drosanthemum floribundum;* 8. Other deep-rooted ground-cover plants recommended by a landscape architect, subject to approval by the Department.

"C. Evergreen Shrubs. 1. *Acacia longifolia* (Sydney golden wattle); 2. *Acacia cyclops* (Cyclops Acacia); 3. *Acacia latifolia* (Broad leaf Acacia); 4. *Acacia armata* (Kangaroo Thorn); 5. *Acacia saligna* (Goldwreath Acacia); 6. *Acacia verticillata* (Star Acacia); 7. *Ceanothus thyrsiflorus* (Blue-blossom ceanothus); 8. *Ceanothus griseus horizontalis* (Carmel creeper); 9. *Eriogonum fasciculatum;* 10. *Baccharis pilularis* (Dwarf coyote bush); 11. *Fremontia californica* (California Fremontia or Flannel-bush); 12. *Cotoneaster dammeri, C. horizontalis, C. microphylla;* 13. *Fremontia mexicana* (Mexican Fremontia); 14. *Grevillea lanigera* (Wooly grevillea); 15. *Jasminum humile revolutum* (Italian jasmine); 16. *Jasminum mesnyi* (Primrose jasmine); 17. *Melaleuca wilsonii* (Wilson Melaleuca); 18. *Nerium oleander* (Common oleander); 19. *Rhamnus californica* (California buckthorn); 20. *Hypericum calycinum* (Aaronsbeard, St. Johnswort); 21. *Rhus laurina* (Laurel sumac); 22. *Rhus integrifolia* (Lemonade sumac); 23. *Rhus ovata* (Sugar sumac); 24. *Rosmarinus officinalis* 'Prostrata' (Prostrate rosemary); 25. *Sollya heterophylla* (Australian bluebell creeper); 26. *Pyracantha fortuneana* 'Graberi' (Graber Firethorn); 27. *Pyracantha* 'Santa Cruz' (Prostrate Firethorn); 28. *Spartium junceum* (Spanish Broom); 29. *Callistemon* (Bottle-brush); 30. *Heteromeles arbutifolia* (California Holly); 31. *Prunus ilicifolia* (Holly-leaved cherry); 32. *Quercus dumosa* (Shrub oak); 33. *Cistus purpureus* (Rock Rose); 34. *Baccharis viminea* (Mule Fat); 35. *Genista sagittalis;* 36. *Garrya elliptica* (Silk Tassel Bush); 37. *Ceanothus oliganthus* (Hairy Ceanothus); 38. *Rhus trilobata* (Squaw Bush); 39. *Eriodictyon trichocalyx* (Yerba Santa); 40. Other deep-rooted plants as recommended by a landscape architect, subject to approval by the Department.

"D. Trees. 1. *Eucalyptus lehmanni* (Lehmann Eucalyptus); (a) *Eucalyptus viridis* (Green Mallee Eucalyptus); (b)

Eucalyptus preissiana (Bell-fruited mallee); (c) *Eucalyptus cornuta* (Yate Eucalyptus); (d) *Eucalyptus megacornuta* (Dwarf Yate Eucalyptus); (e) *Eucalyptus erythronema* (Red flowered mallee); 2. *Schinus terebinthefolius* (Brazilian pepper); 3. *Schinum molle* (California Pepper); 4. *Pinus halepensis* (Aleppo Pine) and other varieties; 5. *Prosopis glandulosa* 'Reese Hybrid' (Mesquite); 6. *Umbellularia californica* (California Laurel); 7. *Cupressus glabra* and other varieties; 8. *Juniperus chinensis* and other *Juniperus* (Juniper); 9. *Juglans californica* (California Black Walnut); 10. *Ceanothus arboreus* (Tree Ceanothus); 11. *Prunus lyonii* (Catalina Cherry); 12. Other trees recommended by a landscape architect, subject to approval by the Department."

Black Mountain list

A less lengthy advisory list has been prepared for the Black Mountain Soil Conservation District (largely the Santa Clara Valley and southern end of the San Francisco Peninsula) by the Soil Conservation Service of the United States Department of Agriculture. This list has no legal standing.

"Shrubs. *Arctostaphylos hookeri* (Hooker Manzanita); *Arctostaphylos uva-ursi* (Kinnikinnick, or Bearberry); *Baccharis pilularis* (Coyote Bush, or Chaparral Broom); *Carissa grandiflora* (Natal plum—*C.g.* 'Nana Compacta' and *C.g.* 'Prostrata' are dwarf ground covers); *Ceanothus gloriosus* (Point Reyes Ceanothus); *Ceanothus griseus horizontalis* (Carmel creeper); *Cistus ladaniferus* (Gum Rockrose); *Cotoneaster dammeri* (Bearberry Cotoneaster); *Juniperus horizontalis* var. Bar Harbor (Creeping Juniper); *Juniperus sabina* 'Tamariscifolia' (Tamarix Juniper); *Pyracantha* 'Santa Cruz'; and *Rosmarinus officinalis* 'Prostratus (Dwarf Rosemary).

"Trees. *Eucalyptus ficifolia* (Red Flowering Gum); *Eucalyptus sideroxylon* (Red Ironbark); *Prunus lyonii* (Catalina Cherry); *Umbellularia californica* (California Laurel).

"Grasses and legumes. Barley; *Lolium rigidum* (Wimmera Ryegrass); Blando Brome-Lana Vetch."

Plants for steep slopes

The following plants are recommended in Sunset's *Lawns and Ground Covers* as good choices on slopes exceeding 25° where they are to serve as ground covers (or shrubby ground covers):

Aegopodium podograria, *Ajuga reptans*, *Anthemis nobilis*, *Arctostaphylos uva-ursi*, *Artemisia schmidtiana*, *Asparagus sprengeri*, *Baccharis pilularis*, *Bougainvillea*, *Calluna vulgaris*, *Campanula poscharskyana*, *Ceanothus gloriosus*, *Ceanothus griseus horizontalis*, *Ceanothus thyrsiflorus repens*, *Cerastium tomentosum*, *Ceratostigma plumbaginoides*, *Comptonia peregrina*, *Coronilla varia*, *Cotoneaster adpressa*, *Cotoneaster dammeri*, *Cotoneaster horizontalis*, *Cotoneaster microphylla*, *Erica carnea*, *Erica ciliaris*, *Euonymus fortunei*, *E.f. radicans*, *E.f.* 'Vegeta', *Festuca ovina* 'Glauca', *Fragaria chiloensis*, *Gazania*, *Hedera canariensis*, *Hedera helix*, *Hypericum calycinum*, Ice plant, *Juniperus chinensis* 'Pfitzeriana Compacta', *J.c.* 'San Jose', *J.c. sargentii*, *J. communis saxatilis*, *J. conferta*, *J. horizontalis* and varieties, *J. procumbens*' Nana', *J. sabina* 'Tamariscifolia', *J. scopulorum* 'White Silver King', *J. virginiana* 'Silver Spreader', *Lantana montevidensis*, *Lonicera japonica* 'Halliana', *Lotus berthelotii*, *Lotus corniculatus*, *Mahonia repens*, *Osteospermum fruticosum*, *Pelargonium peltatum*, *Phlox subulata*, *Phyla nodiflora*, *Polygonum cuspidatum compactum*, *Pyracantha*, Roses — Banksia, Roses — 'Mermaid'. Roses—*Rosa wichuraiana*, *Rosmarinus officinalis* 'Lockwood de Forest', *R.o.* 'Prostratus', *Santolina chamaecyparissus*, *Sedum*, *Trachelospermum jasminoides*, *Vinca major*, *Vinca minor*, *Xanthorhiza simplicissima*, and *Zoysia tenuifolia*.

Plants that grow up

Where the bank slopes up, these plants can be started at the bottom and left to grow toward the top of the bank:

Ficus pumila (Creeping fig). This hardy vine has small, dark green, heart-shaped leaves and clings tenaciously to any surface by means of little holdfasts. It is best in light shade.

Hedera. *H. helix* (English ivy) is suitable for covering slopes. It will grow up or down. It is one of the hardiest of the many kinds of ivy.

Ipomoea purpurea (common morning glory). Practically everblooming with flowers of white, red through purple to blue—normally open only in the morning. A rampant grower, difficult to eradicate once started. Requires almost no care.

'Mermaid' rose. Climbing, rapid growing rose with waxlike, leathery, practically evergreen, disease-proof foliage. Fragrant, enormous single flowers of yellow.

Passiflora alato-caerulea (*P. pfordtii*). Large, fragrant flowers are white shaded with pink and lavender; the crown is deep blue or purple. Deep green, leathery, three-lobed leaves. Fast growing, not particular as to soil.

Parthenocissus quinquefolia (Virginia creeper). A reliable, completely hardy, deciduous climber that clings to any rough surface. Large five-parted leaves turn scarlet in fall.

Plants that grow down

When a bank slopes downward from a site, the owner often finds it desirable to plant the top of the bank with vines or sprawling shrubs that will cascade downslope with time. These are candidates:

Jasminum mesnyi (*J. primulinum*). Very hardy vine with long, pendulous, streamer-like green branches covered with sheets of two-inch winter blooming yellow flowers. Very rampant.

Plumbago capensis. Forms a billowing mass of azure blue flowers all summer. Fast growing plant for sunny spots. Hardy at 24°.

Clematis armandii. This is the only evergreen clematis generally available. It has handsome dark green leathery leaves, and sheets of star-like fragrant white flowers. Under favorable conditions, it will grow 10 to 15 feet in one year. Older vines extend 25 to 30 feet. Provide shade at base in all sections. Inland, entire plant should have partial shade. Hardy to 20°.

Gelsemium sempervirens (Carolina jessamine). Hardy evergreen vine with trumpet shaped, fragrant, winter blooming flowers of bright yellow. Rapid but not a rampant grower. It can stand lots of heat.

Lonicera japonica 'Halliana' (Japanese honeysuckle). This familiar vine is vigorous and rapid growing, with fragrant blooms over a very long period. It is tolerant of heat and dry air but needs part shade, particularly around the roots.

'Max Graf'rose. This vigorous trailing (not climbing) rose has dark green, wrinkled foliage and three-inch, bright pink, gold-centered flowers. It is an invaluable plant for bank covering.

Matching plants and soils

Hillsides, like anywhere else, vary in soil composition. The following are some basic plants for common soil conditions on slopes.

Sandy soils. On banks with sandy soil, use plants that root quickly, withstand drought, and have strong stems that resist being covered by drifting sand. Such plants are chaparral broom (*Baccharis pilularis*), saltbush, *Carpobrotus edule*, *Hymenocyclus croceus*, and *Lampranthus roseus*. Although large-leaf ice plants are good for holding surfaces of steep stabilized cuts, their own weight may carry them and the topsoil down in heavy rains.

Sandy loam and loam soils. Sandy loam and loam soils erode easily and dry out readily, but they have good texture and are quite fertile. In these soils you can use plants that are both ornamental and capable of controlling erosion.

On rather steep slopes, both Algerian and English ivy provide a good sheeting effect and hold soil. *Hypericum calycinum*, Hall's honeysuckle, trailing mesembryanthemum, dwarf rosemary, *Ceanothus griseus horizontalis*, *C. gloriosus*, and *Sedum amecamecanum* are good choices.

Heavy clay soils. Heavy clay or adobe soils are usually quite stable, but even they will need plants with sturdy root systems that can work into the fine textured, packed soil particles. Heavy soils are usually cold soils; if your bank faces north, use plants with a shallow root system. Ajugas are particularly good on such slopes. Other possibilities are honeysuckle, wild strawberry (*Fragaria chiloensis*—coastal strawberry—is especially good on steep slopes), ivies (Algerian, Hahn's, English), *Hypericum calycinum*, vinca.

In heavy soil on hot sunny slopes, use ivy geranium, *Hypericum calycinum*, junipers, *Hymenocyclus croceus*, *Lampranthus roseus*, or dwarf rosemary. You can also use *Phyla nodiflora* in combination with higher growing material.

Gravelly soils. In gravelly soils, use plants with long, stringy roots that will penetrate and search for soil pockets and moisture. Shrubby types of plants are best. *Baccharis pilularis*, dwarf and taller types of ceanothus, brooms, rhamnus, *Rhus integrifolia*, *R. ovata*, Matilija poppy (*Romneya coulteri*), buckwheat (*Eriogonum*), rosemary (*R. officinalis*), *Cistus hybridus* (*C. corbariensis*), junipers, and *Plumbago capensis* are well equipped to grow in this type of soil. The large leafed mesembryanthemums and brilliant colored lampranthus (ice plant) are valuable in heavy soils.

Wind-resistant plants

For resistance to wind, and also to drought, look to plants with tough, needle-like foliage. Many are native to Australia, New Zealand, and the Mediterranean areas. A number are gray in coloring—and you will find a collection of these grays makes an interesting hillside planting.

Acacias. Use shrubby types such as *A. longifolia* and *A. verticillata*. One of the more unusual species is *A. cultriformis*, with gray, wedge-shaped leaves and fluffy yellow flowers. Prune to keep them low.

Cistus. Rock rose. *Cistus purpureus*, rose-pink with maroon blotches, and *C. hybridus*, white, are particularly attractive. Adapted to slope planting both along the coast and inland. Will stand dry soil, heat, and wind. Hardy.

Elaeagnus pungens (thorny elaeagnus). This extremely hardy spreading 15-foot shrub makes an excellent screen. Leaves and stems are covered with silvery dots. Has small, white, fragrant flowers, and silver-bronze fruit.

Eucalyptus. The compact blue gum (*E. globulus* 'Compacta') has a naturally low branching habit, is especially adapted to slope planting.

Leptospermum. *L. laevigatum* (Australian tea tree) has been used extensively in California to reclaim sand dunes and to hold shifting soil on hillsides. Its variety 'Reevesii' is similar in foliage, but has a compact habit of growth. *L. scoparium* 'Florepleno', the dwarf double pink flowering tea, is very ornamental. It is a medium height shrub with double pink rosette-like flowers. The Lammerts Hybrids are more dwarf, come in a variety of colors and heights.

Melaleuca. Tough and hardy under almost every adverse condition. *M. decussata* is a 15 to 20-foot shrub with blue-green leaves and lavender flowers; *M. hypericifolia* grows 8 to 10 feet, has brilliant red flowers; *M. nesophila* sometimes grows as a spreading shrub 8 to 10 feet high—if pruned to a single stem, may grow as a 20-foot tree.

Romneya Coulteri (Matilija poppy). Large shrubby perennial growing to eight feet. Gray-green stems and leaves and immense, fragrant, crinkled white flowers. A clump or two highlight the garden all summer.

Rosmarinus officinalis (rosemary). Tall and prostrate forms. Pungent, green or gray-green leaves, and lavender flowers.

Fire-retardant plants

Green ground covers such as Algerian ivy and ice plant have superior fire resistance provided they are irrigated and kept free from too much dry material underneath.

Under regular irrigation and clean maintenance, bamboo, eugenia, palms (if free of dry skirts), and even such reputedly combustible trees as olive, *Pittosporum undulatum*, and pines performed well.

Where irrigation is less easy, another group of plants shows unusual fire resistance and promises some reliability for firebreaks. This group includes: Brazilian and California pepper (*Schinus terebinthifolius* and *S. molle*), California laurel, carob, Catalina cherry, lemonade berry (*Rhus*), and oleander. Naturally, the better irrigated, the better they perform.

Where irrigation is difficult or impossible, four plants under test show high promise. They are Brewer salt bush (*Atriplex lentiformis breweri*), yerba santa (*Eriodictyon trichocalyx*), the rock-roses (*Cistus purpureus* and *C. ladaniferus*), and sun rose (*Helianthemum*). These rival range grasses for resistance to high temperature where flammable brush is removed.

Plants for retaining walls

Many retaining walls need plants that will stand poor soil, lack of water, and general neglect. The following list is recommended by George Schenk in his Sunset book, *How to Plan, Establish, and Maintain Rock Gardens*, as meeting all these requirements and further being made up of attractive plants.

For large walls. *Arctostaphylos media*, *A. uva-ursi*, *Cedrus* (prostrate forms), *Cotoneaster adpressa*, *C. dammeri*, *Cytisus*, *Ceanothus gloriosus*, *Euonymus fortunei* 'Vegeta', *Genista*, *Hedera*, *Muehlenbeckia*, *Juniperus* (prostrate forms), *Pyracantha*, *Vinca*.

For walls less than 6 feet high. *Alyssum saxatile*, *A. wulfenianum*, *Aubrieta deltoidea*, *Cerastium tomentosum*, *Convolvulus mauritanicus*, *Cotoneaster horizontalis*, *C. congesta*, *Daphne cneorum*, *Dianthus gratianopolitanus* and hybrids, *D. deltoides*, *Dryas octopetala*, *Duchesnea indica*, *Erica carnea*, *E. purpurascens* 'Darleyensis', *Erica vagans*, *Euphorbia myrsinites*, *Ficus pumila*, *Fragaria chiloensis*, *F. californica*, *F. virginiana*, *Genista pilosa*, *G. radiata*, *G. sagittalis*, *Geranium sanguineum* in all its forms, *Hebe decumbens*, *Hedera helix* 'Hahn's Self-Branching', *Helianthemum* hybrids, *Hypericum polyphyllum*, *H. olympicum*, *Iberis sempervirens*, *Lathyrus splendens*, *Linnea borealis*, *Lithospermum diffusum*, *Omphalodes verna*, *Penstemon fruticosus*, *Phlox nivalis*, *P. stolonifera*, *P. subulata*, *Polygonum vaccinifolium*, *Potentilla reptans*, *Rubus fockeanus*, *Saponaria ocymoides*, *Saxifraga sarmentosa*, *Sedum album*, *S. rupestre*, *S. spathulifolium*, *S. spurium*, *Veronica catarractae*, *V. pectinata*, *V. repens*, *V. prostrata*, *V. latifolia*, *Viola hederacea*, *Zauschneria californica*, and *Z. latifolia*.

Broad flight *of steps of exposed aggregate welcomes guests at an asphalt parking area, points way to house. At night, Japanese lantern on bordering stone wall and hanging light in the olive tree illuminate steps and path. Big rocks border the steps on the far side. The landscape architect was Warren E. Lauesen. Note extra-wide first tread.*

Steps...they invite guests into a garden

Although the basic function of steps is to get you up and down in the most convenient, practical way, they can do more than just that to make a garden livable.

In the garden, steps free the mind from navigation problems. They extend a welcome, pointing and leading from one area to another. They have their own curious mood and tempo, causing their users to hurry up here, and pause a moment there. They give a stroller a natural, easy pace and rhythm. They do all this *if* they are thoughtfully designed and properly made.

Inexperienced step builders often think the best way to build from one level to another is to let the steepness of the hill dictate the steepness of the steps. This is seldom the case. Too steep, and you will need handrails. Too shallow and your steps may become stumbling blocks in what should be a ramp. In the accompanying chart are shown ramps and steps best suited to four regularly encountered garden situations.

Tread-riser relationship

For successful steps, it is important to get the right tread and riser proportions. The step with bad proportions can bring you down with a shock, and might even twist your ankle. A good proportion for garden steps, midway between ramp and ladder, is a 6-inch riser and a 15-inch tread. Work out from this in either direction as necessity dictates. Other proven proportions are a 5-inch riser and 17-inch tread, a 4½-inch riser and 18 inch tread, a 4-inch riser and 19-inch tread. A rule to respect is that twice the riser plus the tread should equal 25 to 27 inches.

If you are working within fixed points, such as between house and garden path, your choice of tread and riser combination is limited to what will fill the available space. But you need not use a bad combination just because it fits. Fit a difficult slope by breaking the steps into flights and landings, or by curving the path of the steps, or by zig-zagging.

Risers *of near steps extend to form terraced planting bed, second flight of steps. Eckbo, Royston & Williams.*

Curving brick *steps course between walls of broken concrete laid dry. Plants add to soft feeling.*

Steps made *with blue slat treads and redwood risers, edged with large boulders, make natural looking transition leading up to curving path barely visible through trees in background. Landscape architect: Peggy Sullivan.*

Cast concrete *squares supported by wood risers. Plant boxes are wood. Landscape architect: Kathryn Stedman.*

Steps look *bigger than they are because treads flow into planting beds at one side. Landscape architect: Kathryn Stedman.*

Varying lengths, *generous proportions, contrasting materials make pleasing steps. Landscape architect: Burr Garman.*

Switchback *eases the climb up this steep, cut bank. Steps are concrete cast in place with redwood risers. The ground cover is small-leafed iceplant.*

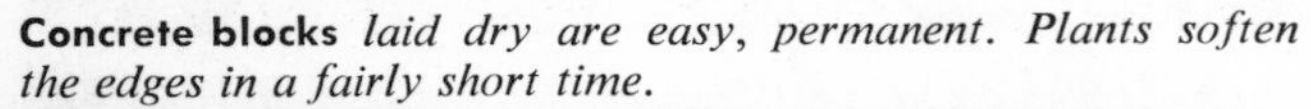

Concrete blocks *laid dry are easy, permanent. Plants soften the edges in a fairly short time.*

Red clay tile *treads, redwood risers make this flight of steps from carport down to patio attractive. Short flights make them inviting. Landscape architects: Eckbo, Royston & Williams.*

Rough redwood *planks are informal, with ivy growing in the riser spaces. Landscape architect: Geraldine Scott.*

How wide? *The sketch at left shows some minimums: For two people side-by-side, 4 feet is the least; additional width increases the importance of the steps. At right, utility steps. Two feet is enough for one person with no equipment. Three feet is better.*

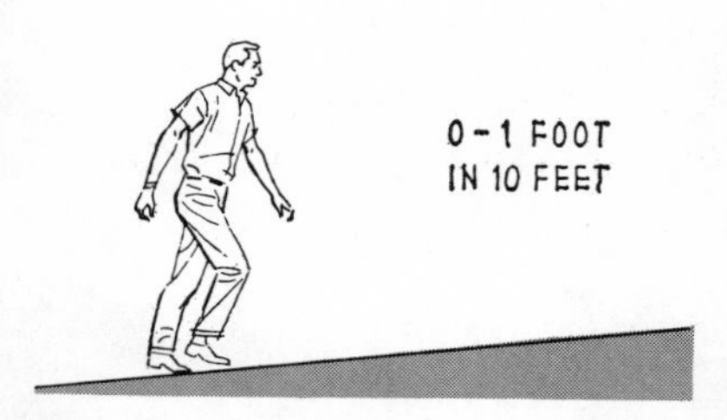

A ten *per cent rise is maximum for long pushes with wheelbarrow. Unstepped ramp best for such slopes.*

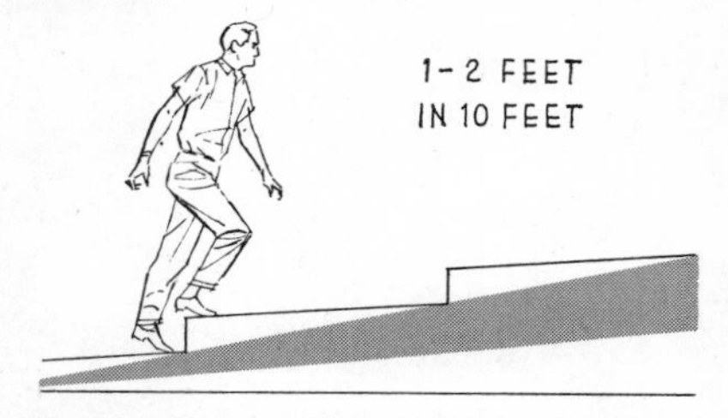

Up to *2 feet in 10 is still too shallow for steps, but is right for stepped ramp with two strides between steps.*

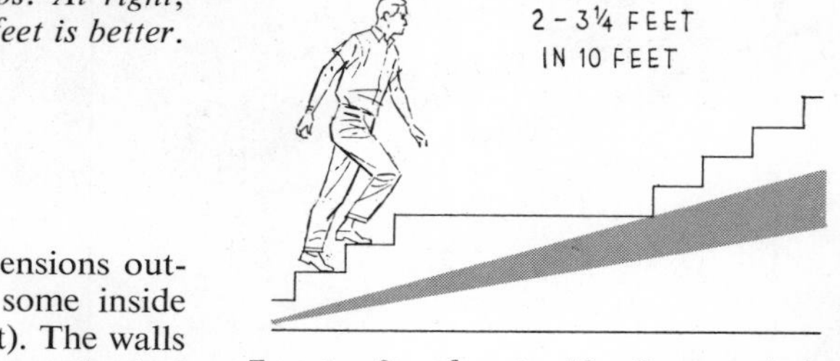

Two to *3¼ feet in 10: Steps-and-platform combinations give wide choice of design. Keep tread-riser ratio in mind.*

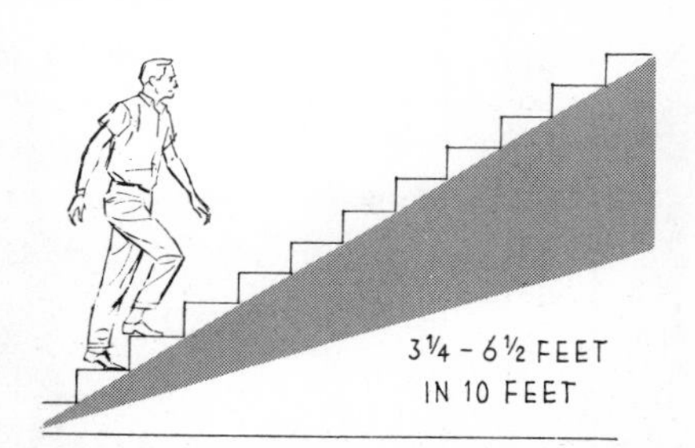

Only steps *on slopes of from 3¼ feet in 10 (6-inch riser, 15-inch tread) to 6½ feet in 10 (7-inch riser, 11-inch tread).*

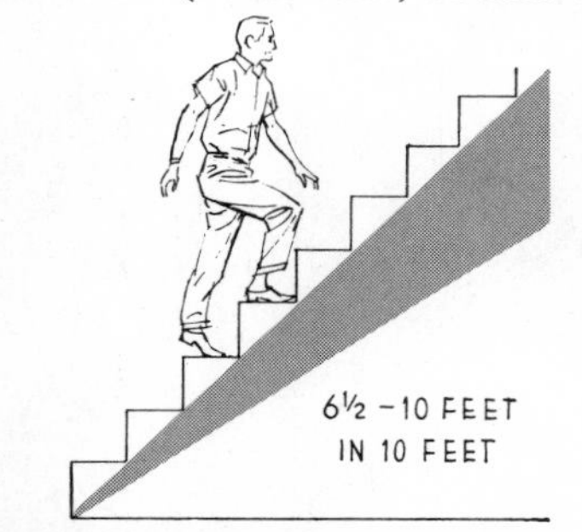

Anything steeper *than 6¼ feet in 10 is all right for the cellar, but it is not good in a garden.*

The psychology of steps

How do steps relate to the rest of the garden? You can make them its most important design factors. If they are narrow, or concealed by walls or hedges, they can separate two areas. If wide, they can bring areas together, and act as a retaining wall as well. If they project toward an area, they can guide your eye and your feet to it. If they curve in a convex arc, you have a range of directions to follow down them. If concave, they give the eye a focal point near the center of their arc.

In the sunlight, steps can throw strong, horizontal shadows to give a base to the verticals of house or trees.

Some basic dos and don'ts

Break up long flights of steps with landings. A long steep flight of steps can give you a feeling of exhaustion even before you start up.

Do not make treads narrower than 11 inches, and treads that narrow are better avoided even if it costs. For the old and very young, low risers present fewer problems than steep ones. But for whatever age, the closer steps come to allowing a normal walking stride, the safer and easier they are.

Do not bring inside dimensions outside (see pages 66-67 for some inside dimensions not to bring out). The walls and balustrades that give you physical and moral support on a stairway do not exist in a garden. On the descent, steepness can be dangerous. And walking and working in the garden, you are almost always carrying something, often with both hands. However, if you make steps too shallow you will find yourself taking them two at a time.

Make garden steps wide. They will look better in the outdoors, and will have room at the edges for garden growth to overlap and soften their lines. Steps make good seating too, as witness the amphitheater. Generous width will encourage their use as seats.

Prevent rain or garden water from standing on the steps by giving the treads a slight pitch, not more than ¼-inch per step. If the step has an open riser, it is better to tip the step to the rear for safety.

Do not worry about perfect finishing. All but the most formal gardens will tolerate a surprising amount of "hand hewn" detail.

If the steps are used often at night, install a lamp that casts light down onto the treads (but not up into a person's eyes). As an additional measure of safety, paint white strips on the leading edges of risers to increase their visibility.

Floating platforms *of 2 by 3-inch decking mount to entry. They are supported on steel pipes set in concrete footings. Landscape architect: Joseph Yamada.*

Similar steps *to those at left have an even airier quality because they do not go up so quickly, but rather serve as a bridge over small gully.*

Notches *cut into a 4 by 20-inch beam support treads of this simple stairway. Wrought iron rail is painted black. Architect was Van Evera Bailey.*

Telephone pole *is the center column for spiralling flight of wood stairs leading to old home. Risers are 2 by 6-inch lumber. Treads are 2 by 10-inch lumber.*

Aboard an incline elevator

Time was when almost any residential elevator you saw was installed indoors to aid invalid or elderly persons. But today we see an increasing number of incline elevators installed outdoors, and not just for invalids. Many are used simply to make a steep site more accessible, and because they are fun to ride.

A form of cable car, these incline elevators are electrically powered, and driven by cables, chains, or cogs. They have push-button controls at each landing and in the cars. Most of them travel about 50 feet per minute. They are about as foolproof and maintenance-free as a public elevator and they have good safety equipment, including slack cable and broken-rope devices and automatic brakes.

The moving-chair elevator shown in the center column is limited to a run of 25 to 40 feet. But the cable car type can have a much longer run (one in current operation has a 1,000-foot track).

The cars driven by cables run very smoothly and almost without any sound. The same cars can be driven by chains, with a bit more noise and slight jerkiness.

The advantage of chain types is that they can be set up by inexperienced men.

A one-passenger chair elevator with 25 feet of run costs about $1,800 installed (a figure which does not include covered landings, almost a necessity with this type). A two-passenger chair costs about $2,500 in a similar situation. A two-passenger car with chain drive, on a 100-foot run on a 30-degree slope, costs about $4,000 installed, complete with landing platforms. A similar four-passenger car with cable drive costs between $5,000 and $6,000, complete with platforms.

These costs are general estimates. Each site poses its own special problems. Material investment can be substantially reduced by choosing a monorail model over a two-rail model when conditions permit.

When these cars permit the use of otherwise inaccessible building sites (and therefore lower cost sites), they can represent an economy. This is only if building costs are not higher than usual because of the site.

When built for an invalid, the expense of installing an incline elevator may fall under tax write-off regulations.

San Francisco *cable car was the inspiration for external appearance of this incline elevator which links house with pool set on terrace far below. It is a four-passenger model and uses a cable drive. Cabin is custom-built.*

Moving chair *types work best if landings are sheltered from the weather; otherwise they work well outdoors.*

Garage *and garbage pickup far downhill from house led to this specially adapted incline elevator. Slope is 37°.*

Pools...they are easier to build now

Excavating *allowed pool to be set deeper into hillside, leaving more room for terrace in design by Armstrong & Sharfman. Terrace is lower than pool, so landscape architects added a small deck for sunning directly at water level.*

As with many other aspects of hillside construction, swimming pools have advanced from a forbidden subject to a state of relative enlightenment. Difficult hillside situations have been tackled and conquered, and the results are often very striking. The successes are due both to improvements in design and construction, and to the wide variety of pool materials available. You can get a good idea on the practicality of a pool on your particular site with the report of a soils engineer and preliminary report of a pool engineer.

The pool, itself, may be constructed of concrete, steel or vinyl:

• **Concrete.** This is the most common type of flat land pool, but its use on hillsides is somewhat limited. A concrete pool must be securely anchored in firm soil, have walls thick enough to handle the excess weight of the earth on one side and make up for lack of support on the downhill side, and be protected from extra pressure by elaborate drainage systems.

• **Steel.** Where there is no outside support (for example, out over a ravine or on a very steep lot) then steel is the only possibility. The pool often will resemble a post-and-pier house, since it requires the same long legs and concrete anchors.

• **Vinyl.** This is the most versatile material. The round portable pools that are sold primarily as above-ground backyard units can often be dropped into a deck to make a very striking outdoor living area. The vinyl liner usually is contained in an aluminum frame that is strong enough to hold in the water and can be easily tied to the deck frame. Larger vinyl liners can be fitted to steel frames for steep hillsides where an extensive deck is impractical. There is a wide range of sizes and shapes.

Steep slopes *can sometimes be overcome with relatively inexpensive deck built out over the slope while the pool is located on a small terrace or naturally level spot, as landscape architect Anthony Guzzardo did here. Sauna on deck.*

On steep slope, *there was not enough flat space for sunning around pool, and main patio terrace was too distant, so landscape architects Eckbo, Royston & Williams added a deck out over the pool. Headers in patio concrete extend as deck beams.*

At foot *of slope was long, narrow trough. Landscape architects Armstrong & Sharfman put pool at one end, then play yard (fenced off), and carport at far end. House just to right of pool.*

Stark flat *space of pool and terrace is broken by raised planting beds which help lead eye up to slope beyond. Low retaining wall on far side. William Kapranos was the landscape architect.*

Outer half *of pool is on fill (the oval shape adds strength); outer wall is massive retaining wall. Architect John H. Ostwald added dramatic bridge to enhance sun deck (see below).*

Vinyl liner *in aluminum tank allows swimming at this hillside home. Deck surrounds pool, which was designed by owner. See detail photo below, right.*

Deck *of pool shown above is cantilevered out from retaining wall. Facer on beam ends presents clean line.*

Steel tank *on steel posts allows small pool to rest entirely free of slope. Architect was Raphael Sampson.*

Aluminum tank *in heavily braced wood frame holds pool shown above. Pool rests entirely free of slope.*

Separate play yards are mutually rewarding

Play space for children on hillside sites is not always easy to come by, but conscientious planning can turn up some delightful surprises for families with children.

First, a sloping garden almost requires that activities be separated from each other, a great boon when the kids want to capture some legendary outlaw at the same time father wants to sit in peace on his patio at the end of a business day he did not enjoy all that much.

Second, banks and slopes offer some opportunities for play equipment that cannot be duplicated handily on the flat.

Terraces and decks are the usual responses to the need to separate a children's play area from other outdoor living spaces. In addition to the ideas shown here, see examples on pages 24-25 and 30-31.

If the children do play on decks, there are a few points to watch. First, railings should be stout and should be covered with a screen tightly woven enough so it does not offer a toehold to tiny climbers. Second, spacing of the deck boards should be tight enough so small toys, crayons, and marbles will not fall through. Third, glass windows or doors should not extend low enough to be hit a forcible blow by wheels or handlebars if wheeled toys are permitted on the deck, or else play should be confined to an area of the deck where glass does not extend to floor level.

If you install sand boxes or other wall-enclosed play areas, you might make the original design with an eye to converting them to raised planting beds after the children have graduated to more sophisticated gamesmanship.

This 12-foot slide *uses hillside and 6 square feet of level space. It is framed of common grade 2 by 2's, 2 by 4's, and 2 by 6's. Sliding surface is ¼-inch tempered hardboard, cross-braced every foot. Tanbark landing pad.*

Tree house tower *is good device if you lack level space. Children can swing, climb, camp out.*

Adventurous *variation on slope-fitting slide is this dragon, made of barrels welded end-to-end. Tire is mouth.*

Step-and-slide *combination works fine on hill garden between parking area and entry. Design by Eric Armstrong.*

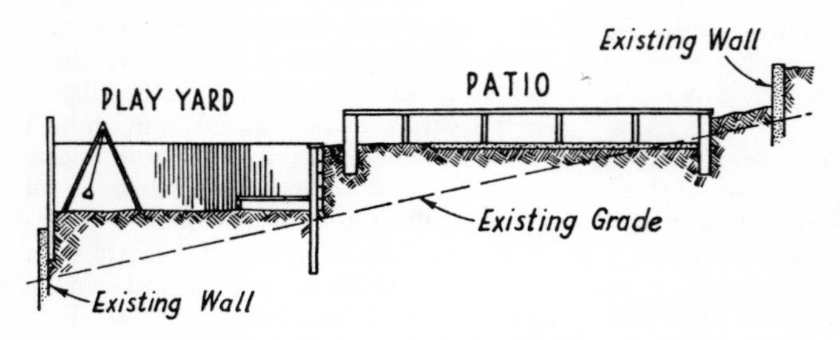

Play yard *is on lower level, adults' patio on upper level. Retaining wall between eliminates need for fence to hide youngsters' play equipment. Design, Osmundson and Staley.*

Flat area *between house and driveway was just big enough for a playhouse. Three fence panels hide it from the driveway and street at bottom of steep bank.*

Four-foot *grade drop between house and garden was bridged by wood deck suitable for play area. Screen at left provides a windbreak and privacy. Douglas Baylis design.*

Porch *is play yard 20 feet wide. It wraps around two sides of house. Translucent plastic overhead provides shelter while letting light through. Architect was James Hosey.*

Carport floor *extends through wall to become a play court. Deck is fenced off to keep it reserved for adults. Sandbox fits against retaining wall below court.*

Solving the problem of parking space

When you live on a hillside you often must contend with steep driveways, sharp turns, and limited level parking space for guest and family cars. Few hillsiders, however, would trade the joys of their site for the easier parking problems of the level lot.

There are no simple or standard ways to accommodate the auto on a hillside. You simply must do the best you can with what you have. The existing streets, the view, the plan of your house, and the size and slope of your lot will determine what you do and where you do it. Convenience for the family and for guests is the controlling factor. Safety is also important.

You will want to get the family cars as close to the house as you can, and as close to the house floor level as possible. We all do an unbelievable amount of carrying from our cars into the house, and there is a real advantage in having the car close and on the same level, especially if you live in a rainy area.

On a very steep hill, the best solution often is to double up on space—to park the car above or under the house. If the car must park on a different level, you are lucky if its location is uphill from the house. Then you won't work against gravity carrying heavy boxes of groceries from car to kitchen.

Guest parking

Guest parking on a hillside is often a luxury. You try first for level parking and garage space for family cars. If you can achieve additional level space for guest cars, so much the better. If a narrow loop drive is to serve for guest parking, guests will have to plan their departure time for a minimum of confusion. Otherwise, guest parking will probably have to be out on the street or else in an adjacent strip.

What about safety? The disturbing thought of a car careening out of control down a hill has bothered practically everyone who has parked on a steep street. The best precaution, of course, is a level parking space. On a slope you may achieve this with cut and fill, by putting a parking deck on posts or on a flat roof, or sometimes under the house.

If guest cars must park parallel on a slope, install a section of solid curb to turn the wheels against. On a gentle slope, a contoured bump and dip for the back wheels will help keep a car in place. Watch that the dip isn't too deep; remember that most imports and sport models have low, low bodies and tail pipes that scrape if the back wheels are much lower than the front ones. Where it is absolutely necessary to park on a steep slope, you can provide chock blocks to go behind the rear wheels.

Good visibility is important in the parking area, drive, and intersection with the street. If possible, avoid sharp turns and blind corners. Here, too, if there is enough space available provide a level turnaround at the end of your drive so guest cars won't have to back into the street.

Hillside car handling isn't all problem. There are advantages as well. You often get exciting structures, and on the hillside you aren't likely to end up with the commercial look of the level parking lot.

When you cut and fill on a steep slope you must consider drainage, settling, slipping, and grade just as much as you would for a house. Some hillside installations have washed out; others have been condemned. If your slope problem is at all severe, it will pay you to consult a qualified engineer. Constructing drives and parking areas on a slope is expensive at best, and can be doubly so if the first effort is done improperly.

This carport *is on two levels to accommodate a steeply sloping street. It avoids a sharp dip or climb. Floor is concrete over corrugated iron. Design, Dennis & Whitaker.*

If there *is no room for a deck, the roof of the house may serve. Back wall of house is concrete retaining wall. Angled baffle is for privacy on sun deck.*

Four cars *can park here, and there is provision for a sunny sitting area (over house roof) as well. Plants in containers to be added, along with patio furniture. Skylight cluster in house roof serves interior rooms.*

Metal railing *provides security without adding bulk. Deck is laminated 2 by 4's set on edge. Tire stop is 6 by 6. Architects: Knorr-Elliott & Associates.*

Steel legs *hold this parking deck high above the slope. It is just below road level, and is tied to a continuous concrete footing. Architect: Joe Davis Allen.*

On a steep *site above the street, grading left a retaining wall. Architect David Thorne used it to anchor carport roof, which shelters steps up to house.*

Level space *is paved near street level to make a turn-around, save drivers having to back into busy street. At foot of bank, it is not visible from the house.*

Steps *in center of uphill driveway relieve its appearance. Landscape architects Armstrong & Sharfman solved lack of entry stair space in this novel fashion.*

On the uphill *side of the street, a Y-shaped drive leads into under-house garage and also provides guest parking or an ample turn-around.*

Gardening on Hills

In Seattle, there is a lush garden planted on a slope so steep that the owners had to lower themselves on ropes to prepare the planting pockets and to set out the plants.

Happily, most hillside gardeners can work their soil, or enjoy the fruits of their labors under less taxing conditions. But that garden does make the point that hillside plantings are special cases.

Soil preparation is in many cases necessary, where erosion or grading has removed the topsoil, leaving only impoverished sub-soils or worse behind.

Special watering devices must be designed and installed to assure ample moisture for plants while also assuring that runoff will not wash dirts (or plants) down the slope.

Hillside gardeners soon learn to use a tray or other device to carry several tools at once, so they won't have to clamber up and down the slope five times to do a single job.

But they also learn that their sites offer some special advantages. Slopes create micro-climates that allow the growing of tender plants at the tops of banks while the same variety cannot endure the frosts at the foot of the hill. Too, slopes allow more flowers—especially the low-growing ones—to be viewed up close.

The stories connected with the photos are to be found as follows: top photo, page 118; next photo, page 111; third photo, page 116; and bottom photo, page 112.

Drainage...the first consideration

Probably 57% of good garden development is in the field of hydraulics, handling water in motion. The steeper the slope, the more critical this aspect of gardening becomes. You create a problem in hydraulics when you put up a roof, and you add to it with each walk, patio, driveway, or other hard surface you install. You complicate the hydraulics when you cut into a natural slope, create a fill by depositing dirt elsewhere, or even when you remove native vegetation.

When your neighborhood was still untouched by man, chances are that rainwater was absorbed mostly by soil. Now, roofs and paved surfaces collect the water that would have been absorbed and concentrate it in small areas so that the soil can no longer absorb it. The untended results are runoff, erosion, and flooding.

Garden engineering is mainly a matter of repairing damage done. The tasks often involve hard labor, or considerable cost, or both. However, every drain tile, every pipe, every concrete pour, every piece of lumber may repay you many times over if the result is a stable slope graced by healthy, attractive plants.

One practical piece of advice about garden engineering right at the beginning: When on your own, tackle only those jobs where failure is of no consequence. As an amateur, you can do many things to assure proper garden conditions. As an amateur, you may attempt major alterations and wind up in the worst kinds of legal difficulties with outraged neighbors, and with the most expensive kinds of damage to your own house and site. Hardly anything is as potentially disastrous as knowing a little bit, but not enough, about hydraulics and soils engineering.

The accompanying photographs of surface and sub-surface drains should be studied in connection with bank planting, terracing, retaining walls, and other sections in the landscaping chapter. The whole subject contains inter-related (and

Textbook example *of drainage problem and its solution. Water from several lots tended to collect between two houses, and in front garden of one of them. To make gardens livable, landscape architect Lawrence Halprin designed drain system that collects water from higher lots (at retaining wall in background of large photo) and channels it between two houses through drain of 6-inch agricultural tile set in ditch two feet deep. Tile packed in gravel to depth of one foot, and overlaid with roofing paper to keep out silt (photo at lower right). Houses on each side of the low spot have foundation drains and roof drains tied into this main channel (upper right photo), which leads to the street. Nine families shared expense.*

Berm at top *of slope doesn't need to look like parking lot curb to do proper job of keeping water off slope. This one, code-required, designed by landscape architect Jocelyn Domela.*

Downslope *runoff, a problem alongside many driveways, can be handled by a gravel-filled surface drain that ties into street storm drain system. Culvert continues this drain.*

At foot *of bank, a stream that is dry but decorative in summer, active in winter. Drain line leads from sump.*

Downslope *surface drainage carried off by brick walk with edges higher than center. A. Arthur Nickman design.*

Flume *needed to drain some banks. This one made of three 2 by 12's with top grate of 1 by 1's. Jack Littlefield design.*

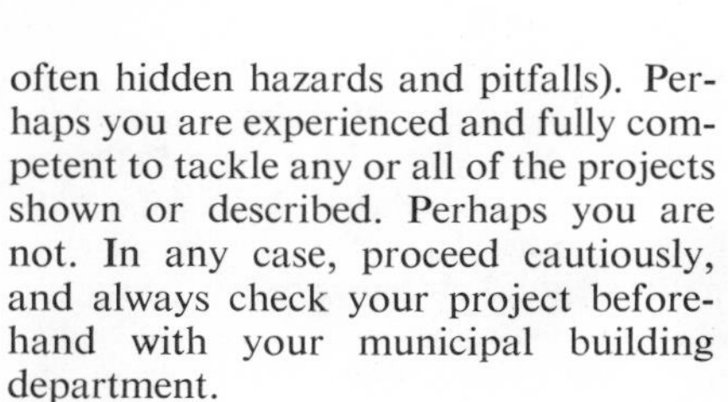

often hidden hazards and pitfalls). Perhaps you are experienced and fully competent to tackle any or all of the projects shown or described. Perhaps you are not. In any case, proceed cautiously, and always check your project beforehand with your municipal building department.

Types of drains

Conditions on the site or code requirements usually dictate which type of drain a homeowner can install.

Where the choice is between a drain line leading water off the property and a sump (or dry well), the former is almost always preferable.

Sumps can handle only a limited amount of water; once the soil around them is saturated they cease to work at all. Where rainfall occurs in short but violent storms, sumps work well to drain low, boggy spots. Sink an 8-foot length of perforated drain tile vertically, and fill it with large-mesh rock.

To move water off the property, there is a choice between surface and sub-surface drains. Surface types usually take the form of dry streams or flumes. Water should never be turned loose from a surface drain until its force has been diminished by some type of baffle, sump, or other device.

Sub-surface drains are constructed as shown on the facing page.

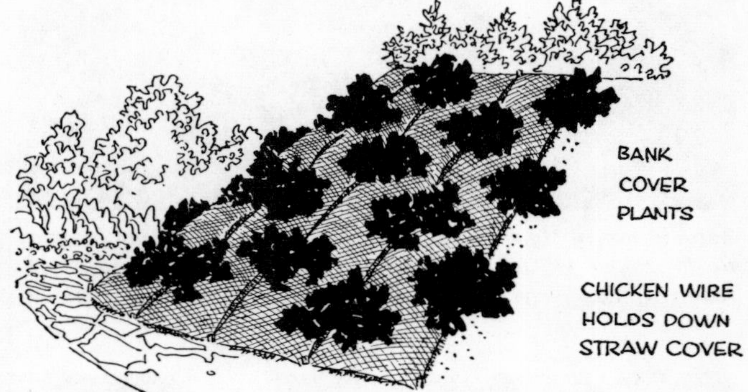

Preparing *a bank requires some care. These methods may help young plants get started. Top left, small furrows are good for seeds or seedlings; the notches prevent washing away. Top right, chapparal wired to deeply driven stakes or rods holds slope while young plants gain footholds. Lower left, a series of metal edging strips holds soil in place on a slope planted to lavender-flowered lantana. Lower right, chicken wire or other mesh holds slope between young plants.*

How to prepare and plant a bare slope

What to plant on slopes is examined elsewhere in this book. When and how to plant are the concerns of this section.

For best growth, the ideal time to plant slopes is in the early spring months, after the heavy rains. It is possible to plant later, but plantings set out too late in the season may be damaged by both early frosts and fall rains before they have an opportunity to take good hold.

Never plant in unstabilized soil. Unstabilized soil is an open invitation to erosion. Also, plants and seeds take hold less readily in loose soil.

Loose fills should be compacted enough to prevent settling, either with hand tamper or a compressor-operated tamper. Fill soils should be placed in layers with proper moisture content and compacted as built up. Steep sites that have been compacted with a sheepsfoot roller behind a heavy tractor usually have loose fills remaining on the sides where they could not be reached by the equipment. Settle the soil by repeated light sprinklings or with hand or power-driven compressors.

Another way to handle the loose fill is to make contour furrows along the slope. Place them at an angle that will allow each furrow to act as a drain to the lowest point at one side of the fill. After watering compacts the furrow enough so it is settled, you can plant in the bottom.

When putting ground covers under trees on slopes, use drought-resistant material, as the tree roots will take most of the available moisture. Also, trees should not be subjected to excess moisture.

Most trees and shrubs have a tendency to lean down the slope as they grow, so be sure to prepare an individual terrace or level area for each ornamental plant. After planting, tie each plant to a strong stake (especially in windy areas). If stakes are not used, let the plant lean slightly upslope.

Any tree, shrub, ornamental, or non-native ground cover will grow more readily if it is planted in a prepared pocket. In all but a few rare cases, steep slopes can be expected to have rather poor soil. To offset this deficiency, add large quantities of humus to the soil in each plant pocket and fertilize.

An exception to the above occurs in the case of natives. Most native plants are harmed rather than helped by manure or other fertilizing. In the case of natives, good drainage is of considerably more importance than good soil, although the addition of humus is usually beneficial.

Avoid digging a sump type hole and filling it with a small pocket of rich soil bordered by compact, hard soil on all

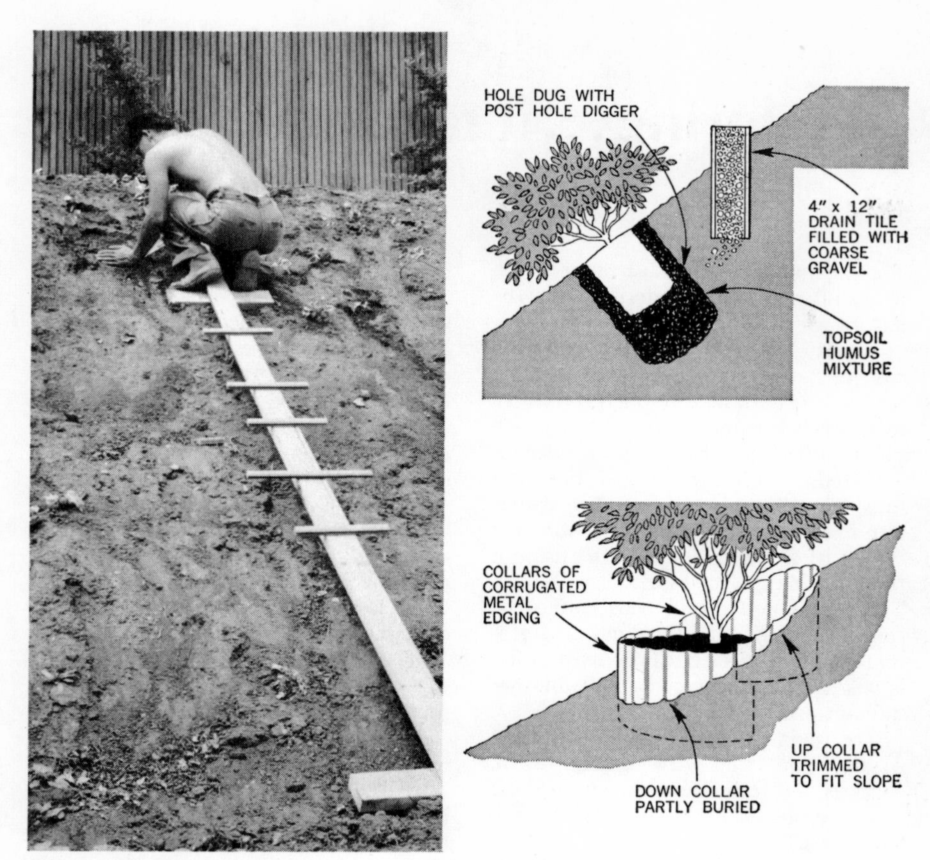

Setting out *individual plants. A ladder makes the task safer, and encourages more attention to each individual plant pocket. Top right, a way to guarantee ample water. Lower right, a different approach, which also prevents silting. Humus, bit of bone meal should go in each hole.*

sides. Provide a transition zone of mixed new and old soil so plant roots have a chance to grow outwards. At the same time, assure good drainage in a prepared pocket. (Fill the newly-dug hole with water and see if it drains.)

Stopgap controls

Stopgap erosion control is a frequent necessity in new gardens or in gardens undergoing an extensive remodel. Here are several proven methods for holding banks with no plants or with only a few new plants.

• If you don't have time to get plants started and their roots established before winter rains begin, you can keep soil from washing out by spreading black plastic over the entire bank after the first rains have thoroughly moistened the ground. Secure the plastic with rocks or boards so that winter storms will not blow it away. A fringe benefit is that this method kills many weed seedlings by shutting out all light.

• If you do have time to establish a temporary cover of plants to be removed later, these are good candidates:

Alyssyum is practical and attractive in mild winter areas. Dwarf Carpet of Snow, Lilac Queen, and Violet Queen are effective, and combine well;

Dimorphotheca (annual African Daisy) likes cool culture, so can be sown successfully in the fall. With careful watering it can be sown at any time except wet winter months. It reseeds itself almost constantly;

Linaria maroccana (baby snapdragon) is best sown in fall or early spring except in cool coastal sections where any time is good enough;

Stable bedding straw is an automatic method. Scatter straw and let rains (or artificial sprinkling) germinate grass and weed seeds, which provide a green cover crop. Later this can be dug or machine-tilled in.

• To protect a lawn on a slope, lay heavy jute netting over the soil after seeding in the normal manner. The netting comes in 50-inch wide rolls, and has a ¾-inch mesh. It resembles a hairy fish net. Secure it at 3 or 4-foot intervals with staples formed from 12-inch lengths of wire. Roll or tamp lightly to work the netting into direct contact with the soil. In addition to controlling erosion, the jute acts as a mulch.

To plant seedlings or sets, prepare the soil, secure and tamp the netting in place, and use a pointed stick or gardener's trowel to widen the loose mesh openings of the jute where you wish to plant.

The material does not have to be removed. The mesh is loose enough for seedlings to grow right through it, and it disintegrates in three or four months.

• Paper netting is surprisingly strong for being made of twisted paper string. There is a large mesh version (½ by 2-inch opening) usually stapled down over a mulch layer of straw or peat moss spread over prepared soil. This is superior for planting extremely steep banks.

A more closely-woven version (¼-inch mesh) can be put down without mulch, in the same fashion as jute netting.

Paper netting also decomposes in place.

• Paint spray, or elastomeric polymer emulsion spray as it is called by the people who make it, is a special formulation of a water-mixed plastic paint which you can spray on a prepared and seeded bed. It dries in about an hour to form a very thin covering film that binds the soil's surface to resist rain and wind. Porous, it allows water to descend through, yet reduces evaporation. Grass seedlings sprout up through the coating without hindrance. Eventually it disintegrates.

Several other chemical formulations do similar jobs. All can be applied with small compressor-sprayers.

One thin coating will not resist the run-off from a storm drain. In areas of heavy drainage multiple coats for strength will not hinder plant growth. A gallon covers about 500 square feet.

• If permanent plants are in, but not grown enough to withstand erosion on their own, good old chicken wire can be used in much the same way as the nettings described above. It can be removed (a tough task), or left in place to rot away over the span of a few years. The choice may hinge on how the bank is to be used. It needs a straw mulch beneath it the first time around.

Weed a permanently planted bank each spring. It removes a potential summer fire hazard, and increases dry-season water supply for permanent plants.

IF SOIL IS COMPACT, LITTLE WATER SOAKS DOWN TO GRASS ROOTS, MOST RUNS OFF AND IS WASTED

Watering...it takes more time

AERATE SOIL, PUT SOAKING DEVICE AT TOP OF SLOPE, LET WATER SEEP OUT SLOWLY

Regular use *of coring device or even pitchfork will aerate sloping lawn.*

The hillside gardener must be prepared to spend more time watering than the flat lot gardener.

Where a slope is left intact or in the case of a steep cut, overhead watering is taboo. It permits too much runoff. In many cases it is necessary to water each plant individually, by the basin method. The basins are fine in summer, but most must be removed or lowered in winter to prevent excessive moisture around the crown of a plant, and thus to prevent fungus and other diseases.

Terraces and raised beds cannot be easily watered with the kind of automatic system so successfully used in flat lawns. Containers can be still another difficult problem.

The main point is to get water deep so main roots will grow deep and firm. Devices and techniques shown on these pages apply to most bank or terrace situations.

Contour irrigation

If you make substantial furrows along a hillside's contours, you can irrigate pole beans, corn, tomatoes, dahlias, and cut flowers without danger of overflow or washout. When water moves slowly, it can soak into the soil, but when it runs off fast, you get little or no penetration. Install a contour system on any unobstructed piece of land that slopes gently enough to walk up (not a hill you *climb* up). Limit this system also to hillsides where soil is deep (not just a thin veneer). Furrows that run along a hillside's contours should follow a 1 to $1\frac{1}{2}$ per cent downgrade. This is just enough fall to keep water moving slowly, yet not enough for fast movement. The 1 per cent fall is for heavy soil that takes water slowly; the $1\frac{1}{2}$ per cent fall is for sandy soil that takes water fast.

You will need a rigid board 12 feet long, a board 6 inches long for one leg, a board 9 to $10\frac{1}{4}$ inches long for the other leg, a bundle of stakes, and a carpenter's level. Nail the 6-inch piece to one end of the 12-foot board. At the other end, nail on a 9-inch leg to make a 1 per cent grade, a $10\frac{1}{4}$-inch leg for a $1\frac{1}{2}$ per cent grade, or any intermediate length if you

Ornamentals *on banks root deeper if water applied with a watering spike.*

Agricultural *tiles sunk in slope are another way to achieve deep watering.*

Terraced beds *can be watered gently by soaker hose strung permanently on wall. Couple regular hose to soaker, which will then release gentle spray all along bed.*

on hilly sites

have a soil that seems to be between the heavy and sandy extremes.

Drive a stake at the highest part of the garden—a spot into which you can run the water. Place the 6-inch leg of the leveling device beside this stake. Put the level on the 12-foot board, near the long leg. Keep the level's air bubble centered, and swing the long board, until the long leg touches ground. Drive a stake there. Move the short leg to the second stake, and swing the device again until the long leg touches the ground. Drive another stake there. Continue staking this way until you reach the end of the garden area. The row of stakes represents an even grade. It may or may not be straight—this is "contour farming." Dig a wide furrow along the row of stakes. Make it up to 18 inches wide for large plants such as dahlias. Plant as close to the furrow's shoulder as you can. If you want another furrow, you can make it parallel to the first one. But if the slope is irregular, parallel lines won't make valid contours; in that case, take another reading.

A series *of watering ponds can take care of an entire slope. Downspout pipes are set in each downhill wall. Careful with trees if you use this* *(see p. 117)*.

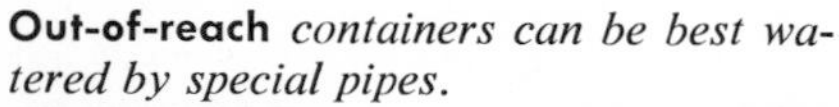

Out-of-reach *containers can be best watered by special pipes.*

Raised beds *can be watered overhead by setting automatic sprinklers up on pipes secured to walls. Full circle or half circle types both available.*

Changing grade near trees

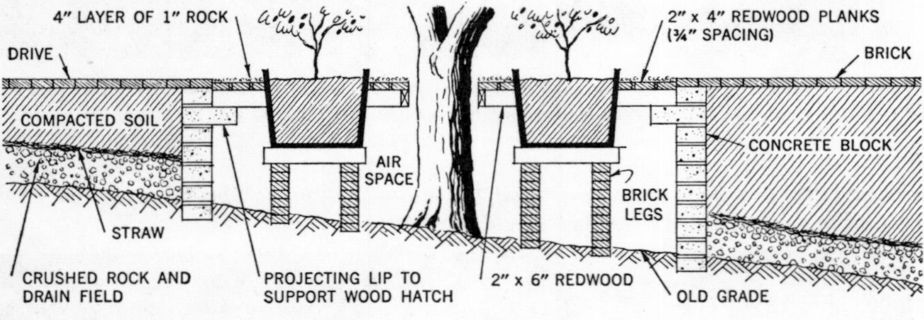

An X-ray view *of the photo would disclose this complicated solution to the problem of saving an old oak. The bricks at foreground of photo are the top of retaining wall that edges driveway. Landscape architect: William Kapranos.*

Need for air *when grade level is raised can often be satisfied with a ring of agricultural tiles laid on original grade level, with vertical pieces reaching up to new grade. Circle need not be complete. The tiles are treated in same fashion as a drainage line (see pages 110-111). Cap with wire screens.*

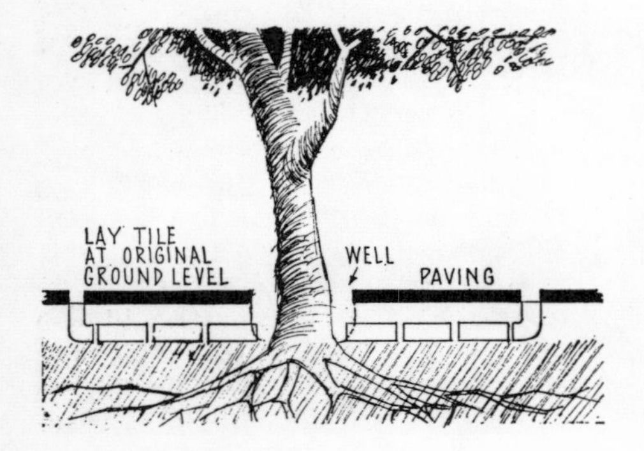

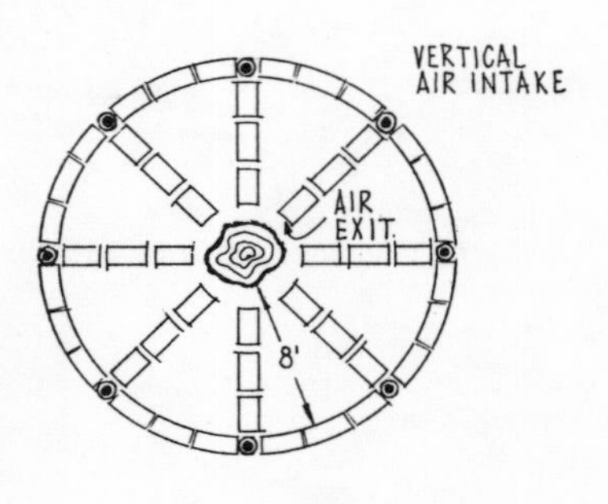

A good many owners of hillside property can look back in sorrow to the death of an old tree so enchanting that it helped them decide to buy the site. In a great many cases, the cause of death was a cut or fill that upset the balance of air, moisture, and nutrients available to the tree's roots.

The best way to keep an established tree in good health is not to disturb the soil above its root zone. Unhappily, this choice does not present itself in every case. Even more unhappily, the alternatives described here hold no guarantee that a tree will survive the period of building and landscaping.

The welfare of an established tree depends on many interrelated factors. Where extensive changes are due, it is usually wise to call in a man from a reputable tree service before the lot is graded. He can judge which trees are worth saving, and knows how to go about protecting them. He also knows how to feed and thin trees that are subjected to grade changes. Tree surgeons, architects, and landscape architects generally agree that preventive measures taken while plans are still in the formative stage show the best results. Remedies applied later cost more and seem less effective no matter who does the work.

On hillside lots, the following points apply widely:

- Although most of a tree's roots are considered to be between the trunk and drip line (outer perimeter of the branches), in many instances roots go much farther. A single tree growing on a dry hillside may have a very wide root system extending four or five times the diameter of the crown, with most of the roots close to the surface and especially vulnerable to any lowering of the grade. (It is a myth that tree roots will travel purposefully to reach moisture; however, where roots reach moisture a concentration of feeder roots usually develops. (Special planting beds sometimes must be lined to keep roots out.)
- The heavy machinery used in grading often presents a hazard in itself. Its weight alone can compact the soil around a tree, slowing down free movement of air in the soil, and preventing normal root penetration and growth.
- Machines and tools working around a tree can damage bark if their operators do not take special care. Injury to the bark may weaken the tree so it cannot adjust to all the other changes taking place around it.
- Landscaping and building often alter the amounts of water a tree gets,

Dry wall *of native rock lines generous well on three sides of madrona, keeps tree at original level, and allows good drainage from a higher level on the slope. Landscape architect was Lloyd M. Bond.*

Special design *of retaining wall by Ruth Patricia Shellhorn preserved an old oak in a large, well-drained well.*

or cause other harmful changes in environment. For example, an often-watered lawn may be put in where there was only a relatively dry slope before. Conversely, a house and paving upslope may reduce the amount of water flowing through a tree's root zone.

• The major calamity for a tree, however, is a significant change in the depth of soil above its root zone. Lowering the grade does the following damage: 1) Exposes feeder roots, causing them to dry out and die, and possibly it severs some of them; 2) reduces the moisture content of the soil by removing the natural mulch on top; and 3) removes the rich, porous topsoil that provides nutrients for the tree. In some cases lowering the grade will lower the water table enough to move water down out of reach of the roots. In extreme cases, enough anchor roots may be severed by grading to allow a tree to blow over during a winter storm.

Raising the grade may be even more detrimental to a tree than lowering the grade. (Raising the grade level just eight inches once killed a number of California live oaks on the Stanford University golf course, but not enough of them to make things easier for high-handicap golfers.) Raising the soil level smothers the feeder roots and increases the moisture in the soil. Such a condition can cause root rot, particularly in heavy soil. Excessive moisture can also cause crown rot, oak root fungus, and water molds.

To change grade levels around mature trees, professionals usually decide on one of the methods described below.

Raising grade level

Where one is possible, a deck at the new level provides an excellent solution from the point of view of the tree. If the deck's surface allows water to drain through, and if there is a foot or more of air space between deck and ground, there occurs very little disturbance of air and water supply to a tree's roots.

Terracing away from the trunk in the gentlest stages circumstance permits is another method that minimizes the changes in environment for a root zone.

Sometimes, a change in grade level will have to come close to the trunk of a tree, requiring a retaining wall or a full-fledged tree well. Some feeder roots will almost certainly smother under the added soil, but the casualty figures can be kept within reason with careful design. Use a light soil with good drainage for the fill. Loamy, sandy, or gravelly soils are about equally good. Remove the layer of mulch from the old grade level before starting the fill; this will compress and become relatively airtight if it decays under a layer of added soil.

In designing a tree well, assure good surface drainage on the downslope side so runoff water is not trapped around the tree trunk, where it creates favorable conditions for crown rot and other diseases. In the same vein, keep the floor of the well clean of bark, twigs and leaves after it is built, and avoid planting vines or ground covers in the well; all of these hold moisture around the trunk. Also, make sure sprinkling systems are designed so they will not spray water into a tree well.

The suffocating effects of a deep layer of new earth can be lessened by placing a ring of 4-inch drain tiles around the tree on an 8-foot radius, as shown in the sketches. Lay the tiles on the old grade level, and go ahead with the fill, making sure that breather holes (at least two) reach the new grade surface.

Solid paving has the same effect as a deep layer of earth; it shuts off a great part of the air and water supply. Loose paving, such as bricks in sand, causes less difficulty than solid paving. If solid paving is used, a tile circle as described above will help restore a balance.

Even if the tile air-supply system is not used, open ground for watering is better placed out near the drip line while paving reaches right up to the trunk. The reason, again, is to keep the trunk dry at grade level where it is most vulnerable to disease.

Lowering grade level

Lowering a grade level may be just as disconcerting to a tree as raising it, but at least the mechanical responses a man can make are fewer and simpler.

Before attempting to save a tree in an area where the grade is to be lowered, be sure that it has roots that go deep. Shallow-rooting and brittle-rooted trees cannot lose a substantial portion of their roots without becoming so unstable that they will topple over without any apparent reason. Nurserymen can tell you whether any tree in question is a

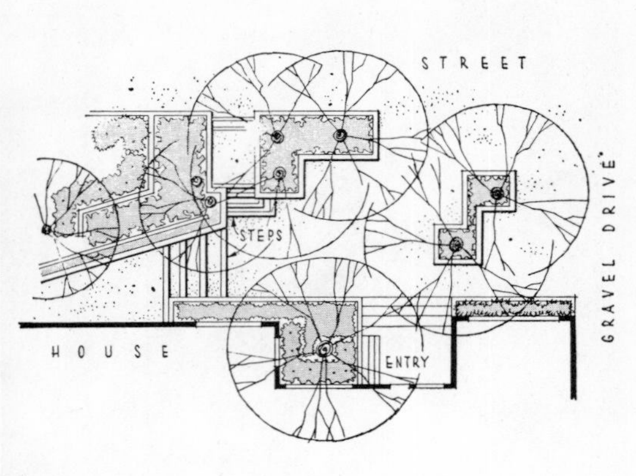

Native oaks *tied a graded shelf to the natural slope around it. To keep the oaks healthy, landscape architect Roy Rydell devised this complex series of raised beds. Excavating near trees done by hand. Note drain holes (lower right).*

Ashlar bond *stone wall circles three sides of bed with ancient spruces. Landscape architect: David Thompson.*

potential danger on this account.

Any tree that loses a substantial amount of root, especially if anchor roots are disturbed, is a candidate for blowing over in a storm. Since the foliage area needs to be thinned to bring it back into balance with the roots, thinning should be designed at least partly to put "holes in the sails."

In some cases clearing off of underbrush will expose a tree for the first time to the full furies of wind storms. With or without an accompanying loss of roots, the trees are endangered. Thinning helps in this case, also.

A retaining wall or a raised bed is the usual answer for trees worth saving when grade level is lowered. A retaining wall near a tree, like any other, should be designed to allow a fairly free passage of sub-surface water, or the accumulated weight will collapse it. In the meantime, the tree roots may rot in the excessively wet soil.

Raised beds should also be designed to provide good drainage. Weep holes near the bottoms of the wall, about three inches above grade, will drain off moisture that would collect around the trunk of the tree encircled by walls of any impervious material.

When the grading takes place, some roots are likely to be cut and exposed. When the cut is completed, cleanly trim the ends of the severed roots and treat them with tree paint. Then cover the exposed soil with burlap or peat moss to prevent its drying out until the raised bed is completed and the roots covered with soil again.

If any part of a root system is lost, the foliage area of a tree should be reduced to bring the tree back into balance. Unless the root loss is severe, an over-all thinning out of small twigs and branches will often do this job adequately.

If a whole branch must be removed because it interferes with a structure, this may re-establish the balance between top and roots.

Make up for loss of roots with plentiful water and food. Combine slow and fast acting fertilizers for a quick stimulant and a continuing supply of food.

Hints for Buyers

Building on a hill removes your home from the ordinary and may even give it some unique qualities. Very seldom will you find many hillside houses that look exactly alike, unless a builder has gone so far as to cut an identical pad for each house and thereby create nothing more than flat lots with sloping sides.

On the other hand, you will rarely find a hillside home without some problems. The buyer who wants a conventional dining L and a simple hall plan should stay off the mountains. The buyer who is tired of orthodox appearances and yearns for some character in his next house will welcome the opportunities that present themselves on steep grades.

For the home builder who has spent all of his days in flat country, it is important to realize the need for a complete master plan. Before the first foot of foundation is poured—and often before the lot is even purchased—the eventual design, building procedure and landscaping should be well in mind. This will save unforeseen expenditures later in the game, and will do away with the immense disappointment that can come if the lot simply does not suit the dream house you visualized.

The stories connected with the photos are to be found as follows: top photo, page 124 ; next photo, page 123; third photo, page 123 ; and bottom photo, page 124.

Agencies to visit

Legal and semi-legal conditions affect every property offered for sale, and potential home buyers often can discover useful information through early visits to responsible local agencies.

Zoning and Master Plans: With the purchase of any new home site, it is wise to familiarize yourself with the master plan and zoning ordinances of the surrounding area. This is particularly true with hillside houses, since the qualities that attracted you to the site may be in jeopardy in future years as high-rise buildings go in, freeways are constructed, and industry expands into the foothills. With the tremendous growth of the West, the hillside house that is now isolated may find itself with hundreds of neighbors within a decade. You will do well to find out in advance just what these future neighbors will be able to do with their land.

Planning Departments: If you are fortunate the area you are exploring will have a city or county general plan, an over-all guide for the community's future. Such a plan is a statement of intention on land use, traffic circulation, and general development. Its aims are to provide residential areas of different kinds that protect health and offer safe, pleasant environment for family living, to provide main streets wide enough to carry their traffic burden without congestion, to locate the civic center where it can be a visible symbol of community life, to place schools centrally within their attendance areas and where small children need not cross busy streets, to prevent factories that may produce noisome effects from locating near homes, and to allow adequate reserves of land for future expansion of the community's productive and commercial activities.

Such a plan is of particular importance to the hillside builder, particularly if he plans to move into an area that is just starting to develop. Area-wide planning is not as easy in hilly sections as it is in the flatlands, and special provisions often must be made for traffic, utility lines and similar services. You may change your original building plans now if you know what the area will be like 10 years in the future.

- Location of future freeways. You will want to know whether a major artery will obliterate your property in the next 10 years or whether it may be a nearby convenience.
- Different types of housing. If you are planning to build on the last remaining lot on a crowded hillside near downtown, look for changing patterns of land use that might allow apartment or commercial use of neighboring land. If you are in a sparsely populated area, try to determine if plans for your neighborhood will eventually include parks, schools and other facilities.
- Annexation. This is a critical area for the person who is building or buying outside of the city limits. You should be able to find out which unincorporated areas are considered within the city's area of interest for possible future annexations. If you plan to move near a city, but not in it, you may have to pay more for the same urban services through special district taxes than you would pay inside the city limits.
- Location of future shopping centers. A few communities, formed to protect their rural character, will permit no commerce now or in the future. But more often, you will find that cities set aside space for future shopping centers as residential areas expand.

The staff of the city or county planning office can also tell you about zoning regulations that will protect the character of the neighborhood and will restrict what you can do with the property. This will include uses of the property (single residence, multiple residence, agriculture), conditional uses (repair yards, recreation, religious uses), height regulations, and minimum lot sizes, widths and setbacks. The latter regulations can be critical in hillside situations, particularly with the irregular boundaries and variations in height that are frequently found. It is a sad owner who thinks he has picked up a bargain in an odd lot, then finds that he cannot build a suitable house because of zoning regulations. Local improvement associations may also impose other deed restrictions not covered or enforced by cities or counties.

A final point worth checking is the number and frequency of zoning violations, variances, special permits and non-conforming uses allowed by the city council or county board of supervisors. If you are attracted to a house on the edge of town because it is near open fields shown on the general plan as an agricultural reserve, the open land may still be turned into a subdivision, factory site, or shopping center unless the council or supervisors are firm in their support of the plan. You can't tell how they will act in the future, of course, but their past record may be an indication.

At the planning office you may also get warning of such future problems as street access, potential traffic generation, drainage from increased run-off, and possible encroachment of facilities needed for growing urbanization—electric power lines and substations, reservoirs, water tanks, flood control ditches, new roads. This, again, is important for the isolated hillside lot that eventually will become part of a larger community.

Here, too, you can check on anticipated subdivision of land. This is especially important where agricultural lands and large estates are slowly changing into areas of smaller home sites. If possible, inquire about possibilities on all the land that is important to your view; the hill a few miles away that makes a beautiful backdrop for your patio will look much different if terraced and stacked with tract houses.

Building Inspector: If you plan to build, you can get building code and zoning information here. If you have any doubts about the suitability of a lot as a building site, many building inspectors will make a preliminary estimate at your request. Some buyers even stipulate in the purchase agreement that the completion of the deal is subject to the examination of a building inspector. If you are concerned about the types of soil on the hillside, you can ask for records of any failures on nearby properties.

Health Department: If the property is in a rural area, you will want to know the availability and limitations of water and sanitation services. These can vary widely from lot to lot in areas outside urban service districts.

Engineer's Office: The city or county engineering staff knows about flood control and special drainage situations that might affect property. You can also find out about access to a public street or scheduled future widening or abandonment of a street. A relatively simple improvement of a road along your property line may mean a new alignment for your driveway, changes in your drainage system to conform to the new contours of the road, and landscaping alterations to block out noise and the stares of passing motorists.

Assessor's and Recorder's Offices: Here you can find out the property's assessed valuation, how this compared with that of nearby properties, and what the tax rate is. The total rate includes those of several jurisdictions—for example, county, city, school and sometimes one or more special service districts.

Site considerations

Hillside development has advanced rapidly as an increasing number of people look to contoured land either out of necessity or because it offers more opportunities for individual expression. Very few hillside projects can now be termed "impossible," if proper steps are taken to make sure the site is capable of supporting a residence and related facilities.

Hillside sites present problems that the flatland developer never thought existed. But the problems can usually be solved with more design and more money, so that your range of available land has expanded rapidly as the architects and builders have sharpened their skills.

The hillside resident who finds himself in difficulty with an unacceptable house or with a back yard that fills with water during winter's first storm and then starts to slide with the second is the one who failed to gather enough information about his problems. Building inspectors and architects both are critical of the buyer or builder who does not know the topography of his site and has not bothered to acquaint himself with the drainage or slide problems that are common to the area.

In most cases, any gradual slope or a steeper grade on solid rock presents no great problems to either the architect or landscape designer. But it is the exception that can cause problems for both the owner and his neighbors. If you have any doubts about your lot or the building inspector expresses some concern over the land as a building site, then a soils engineer can provide valuable information. A soils engineer will take samples and analyze the strata, looking for expansive soils and poor stability. Borings are usually taken to a depth of about 10 feet, and you receive a report that details the situation. From this report, your architect can devise the proper foundation for the house and also build in safeguards against possible slides. Cost for these services is about $100-$300, depending on the lot.

Some cities and counties will require a report from a soils engineer before issuing a building permit. Only a few areas are strict enough to require a report on every hillside site, but almost all reserve the right to ask for this information if they feel the lot may not be a safe building site, or if conditions become apparent after construction begins that warrant soils investigation and redesign.

Judging your particular site by those on either side can be a tricky business. It is true that rock strata usually do not vary from site to site, and that a soils engineer or building inspector may base his report on your land on the evidence available from what has happened to your neighbors. But at the same time, slight changes in contour and degree in slope can have a great bearing on the rock foundation. It is wisest to rely on professional opinion if there is any serious question.

Modification of the natural slope is a debatable issue. In general, the less gouging you do, the better off you will be. But at times, you may not be able to fit a house to the land unless some resculpturing is done. So the best rule of thumb is to do only what is necessary, and don't let a bulldozer blade touch even a blade of grass until you have mapped out a complete grading plan, preferably with the aid of an architect and landscape architect. Above all, don't manhandle the land by clearing off the whole site, eliminating a great deal of natural growth you might like later, making sharp lines out of the gentle curve of the hill, covering topsoil with clay, and baring the hillside to erosion. As the bulldozer cuts a deep swath, it upsets the mountain ecology that has provided the right balance of natural growth and the right type of drainage that probably gave the site much of the appeal that attracted you in the first place.

If you must upset the land, then you must stabilize the new soil. Cuts mean retaining walls to compensate for having removed the "toe" that provided support for the land mass above. Filled areas mean new compaction. Indiscriminate use of fill can bring slide problems during the first heavy rainstorm. If the new fill is dumped on the original grade, like one brick on top of another without any mortar between, the top section will tend to slide when saturated with water. If the fill is keyed into the old grade in a series of steps, the remodeled land will be much more stable.

Fill that contains uprooted trees and debris may appear to be solid at first, but you run the risk of eventual settlement in future years as the organic material decomposes. Such uneven settlement can cause failure in any structures that use the improper fill for support.

Retaining walls are the keynote to stabilizing cut land, and usually they are not jobs for amateurs. Any wall more than three or four feet high, or one that must hold back more than a 36 percent grade requires special engineering. Most cities and counties are not concerned with small walls, but they tend to be very strict in cases where more than one wall is needed to hold back the slope, or there is need for a single high wall. In some cases, only reinforced concrete or steel are deemed suitable materials for the walls that must bear great weights of soil and water.

Above or below a street?

The choice seldom exists in built-up areas, but in newly developing suburban areas or in rural locations a potential homebuyer often can choose between a lot above the road, or one on the downhill side of the street as the street follows a contour.

When the road runs along the face of a hill, a downhill site is the most practical location to build in almost every respect. This is not to say that all good hillside homes are on sites below the road, but rather that you will have an easier time fitting house to lot, building the house, and landscaping the area. Lots on the high side of the road usually require more work and more money to achieve similar results. (In general, prices for high-side lots are somewhat lower than those for similar lots across the street, compensation for the high costs of building.) For some sample solutions of above-the-street building, see pages 8, 40, and 54.

Because of access problems, it is often costly to select an above-the-road lot that is steeper than 3:1 (one foot vertical to three feet horizontal), while a downside site can be markedly steeper without serious inconvenience in this respect.

Regarding living areas and view, an uphill site often requires some extra attention to avoid annoyances. The living area at the front of the house will overlook the street, so it will require some special construction to block out undesirable parts of the view and street noises. If living areas are at the back of the house, they may butt up against the slope. A steep, high slope may block any view on that side of the house. Upslope neighbors may have an unimpeded line of vision into your patio and living room. The view from a site across the street does not have to contend with the road, which makes any editing easier, and neighbors will usually be farther away and in less clear view of your property.

A downhill lot usually can be (but does not have to be) left in its natural slope, and the house set comfortably on a stepped foundation or stilts. With an uphill site, some cutting and grading will be necessary in most cases to keep

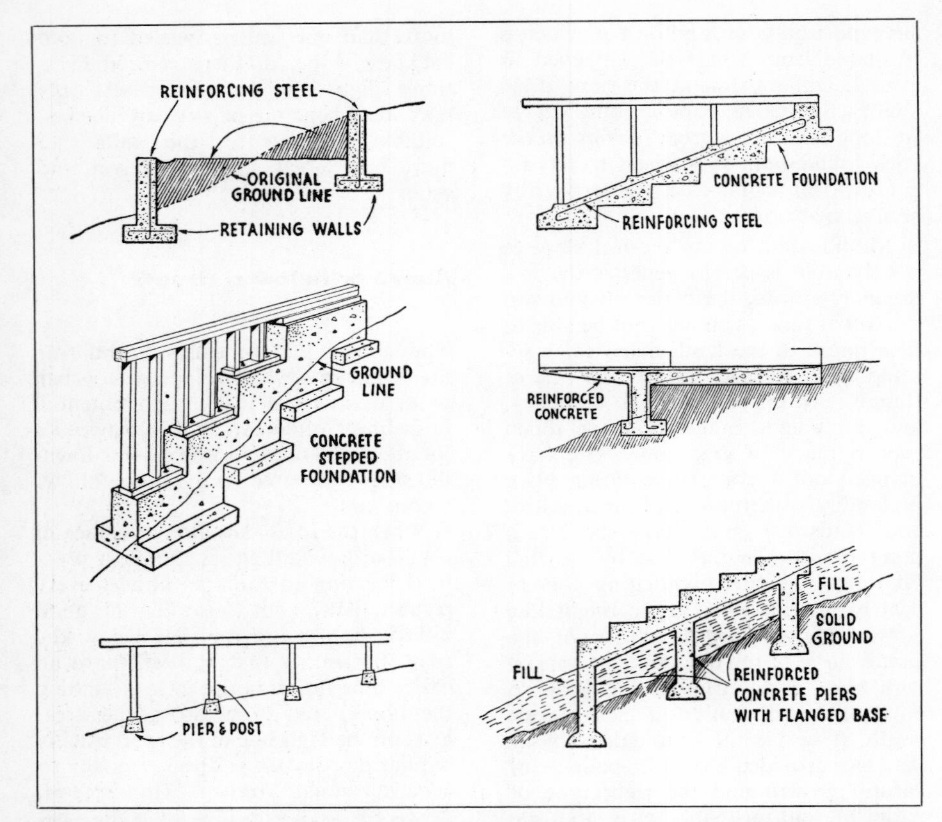

These are *construction methods described in accompanying text. Top left, excavating a level shelf. Walls may not be required. Center left, stepped foundation. Bottom left, pier and post. Top right, platform using a below-grade concrete beam. Center right, cantilever. Lower right, stepped foundation or below-grade beam keyed to stabilize fill.*

the house from towering above its site. To get the house away from the curb the lot must be cut away. To find extra patio space behind the house may require excavation. A large garage or extra guest parking will require some earth movement. The point has been made already that poorly handled grading can destroy the beauty of any lot while introducing new problems of drainage and planting.

Construction materials can be moved down easily from street level to building site by gravity, but materials going uphill may require the use of a power lift. These can be expensive.

A hillside lot offers some natural drainage advantages. Gravity can take most of the water away, and natural drainage channels have been developed with the natural evolution of the hillside. With a downhill lot, it is easier to take advantage of these natural features. The most difficult area is that between the road and the house. Of course every owner should take care that runoff from his property does not damage any property below. On the uphill side, you may have to worry about helping the next neighbor up the hill get rid of runoff water from his property as well as your own, and draining water around your house can sometimes be difficult, especially if there are no storm drains along the road to take care of large volumes of water from your property.

All is not on the debit side of the ledger. Houses on the uphill side of the street usually have little or no open space beneath, which minimizes heating and insulation costs. Also, the owner of an uphill lot can put a fireplace almost anywhere he chooses, while the owner of a downside site may be forced to use a portable fireplace because his floor is too high above grade to make the building of a flue feasible. Most important, the view may be better, and the lot generally more attractive.

Types of construction

There are a number of ways to build a house on a hill. Some are expensive, some are not. Every hillside structure should be planned with the help of a qualified architect, structural engineer, or soils investigator. All hillsides are potential slide areas and the foundations that go on them are tricky. Cutting corners can prove disastrous.

Which design is structurally better for you will depend on the slope of your site and on the soils analysis. Each specific house will require special design, and any one of the types listed here can be engineered to meet building specifications. Even the once-feared house on stilts can be designed safely with the right foundation and proper lateral force bracing.

Excavating a level shelf. This is an expensive type of construction. You not only have the cost of moving the soil, but also the cost of retaining walls to hold the cut and the fill, and, maybe, to hold back your neighbors' property on both sides.

It is necessary, too, when an excavation of this type is made, to run the foundation down through the fill to grade.

It is wrong simply to cut a shelf and treat the whole thing like a level lot. You are likely to end up with a high bank behind the house which is difficult to plant and unpleasant to look upon, and with a deep fill in front which is unstable and easily eroded. Actually, if retaining walls are properly handled as part of the garden plan, they can help mold the house to the hillside.

Excavation does permit the house and some garden area to be on the same level.

Stepped foundation. When properly designed, hillside houses built on a stepped foundation are generally the most satisfactory from the standpoints of cost and strength. The only excavation required is the foundation trenching. You will use more concrete this way, but it will not equal the cost of excavating to a level site.

It is a good idea sometimes to step the house lines with the foundation, so that you do not have a house one story high on the uphill side and three stories high on the downhill side. If you do not step the house, you are liable to end up with a bleak, bare back wall, and a house shape that does not fit the hill.

If you are building on filled land or on adobe soil, you sometimes can save the cost of trenching your foundation to solid ground by using a system of subgrade concrete piers.

A foundation of this type should be worked out by a qualified engineer. He will specify number, location, and design of the concrete piers.

Holes for the piers are drilled through the fill or adobe to solid ground by a drill device similar to that used for telephone post holes.

Pier-and-post foundation. This is in many cases the least expensive method although it still costs more than building on a level lot. It leaves the hillside virtually untouched and props the house up on the hill without apology.

This is a type of construction frequently used for cabin construction in its rough forms, a type which might raise objections with the building inspectors if it isn't properly engineered. At one time the FHA looked dimly upon pier-and-post construction, but improved designs have made such houses acceptable, and in some cases even preferable to other types.

The original objection was that the piers were not as sturdy as a continuous foundation. There are two ways of getting around this, if you like this method for its frank approach to a slope.

One is the below-level concrete beam, which ties all the posts together. At-grade steel beams do the same job for some steel-framed houses.

The other is to sink the posts in concrete caps poured on bedrock. The idea is very similar to the keyed piers shown in the sketch of a stepped foundation, except that it can be even more sturdy than the other method where unfractured bedrock is present within economical reach.

Some experts favor pier-and-post construction in areas of expansive (mainly clays) soils, since soils of this type do not offer a suitable support for continuous foundations.

Another advantage of the method in some cases is that the main platform can be put up quickly by a skilled crew. Regular carpenter crews then have a level surface from which to erect the house frame. Important economies can be effected if this avoids "hazardous duty" pay for carpenters and other building trades crews.

Cantilever construction. Cantilevers require special engineering, massive anchoring, and heavy reinforcement. They are liable to be the most expensive ways to handle a hillside house. Even when properly engineered, you get a certain amount of vibration on the edge of a cantilevered structure. It is not dangerous, but it may upset your sense of security.

But cantilevers have aesthetic values—they have an airy, floating quality that not only adds to the design but gives you the feel of being on a hill. And even though few hillside houses use a cantilever foundation, most of them use cantilever engineering some other way—such as cantilevering a porch, the edge

Post-and-beam *construction using no concrete foundation is sometimes possible. Here, pressure-treated poles are sunk like telephone poles. Architect: Edwin Wadsworth.*

Stressed skin *panels, used with post-and-beam, allow quick, economical construction. Panels are stronger than weight indicates. Design, Gideon Kramer.*

Steel used *here in versatile way. It is main frame of house, and diagonals of steel provide lateral strength, so wall surfaces have no structural function. As result, in this case walls are sliding shoji on three sides of house. Architects: Johnson and Perkins.*

of a deck, or one end of a room. There is usually a practical reason for such a projection, such as cutting off an undesirable view from inside the house.

Drainage

Water that runs rampant across your property can start landslides, break down retaining walls, undermine the foundation of the house, and convert your patio into an unattractive pond. Seepage into basements and garages can be unpleasant and structurally unsound; topsoil washing off down the hill can mean damage to your plants and expensive replacement; water running off your property onto your neighbor's can bring angry complaints.

To install an effective drainage system on your hillside lot, you must determine carefully where the water is coming from, where you want to stop it, and what to do after you have intercepted it. This last factor can be the stickler in many cases. You must consider future neighbors who may not like a culvert dumping into the ravine that is going to be the site of a future deck or patio.

The natural downhill slope of your lot is at once your friend and enemy. It provides the gravity that makes water diversion easier, but it has its own predetermined direction that is sometimes difficult to change. You will have to deal with both surface and underground water, and each has its own requirements. Surface water runs off a slope as from a pitched roof; it is troublesome only during or immediately after heavy rains. Underground water moves slowly through porous layers of earth and may continue to flow many days and weeks after rains have stopped. (You can see this phenomenon when you drive through cuts on many secondary highways; the road will be wet for days after a rain if there are no roadside drain channels.) Subsurface water, by keeping land saturated, prevents surface water from being absorbed and thus causes surface pools and puddles.

Perhaps the most important thing to remember in establishing proper drainage is to keep the water moving, both above and below the surface. If you let it collect and build up great weight and pressure, even strong retaining walls and properly pitched concrete will not be able to hold back the tide. Avoid any bowl effects in the patio or garden where water might collect and super-saturate the soil. If you have a U-shaped house with the wings pointing upslope, the natural bowl that is formed behind the house will need proper run-off to keep the water away from the building. The sod drains should always empty so the water can follow gravity rather than emptying into an uphill grade that will require new diversion channels.

In any hilly area, the city or county undoubtedly has installed some sort of drainage system along roads, or plans to do so in the future. It is your responsibility to include these public improvements in your long-term plans and not block any of the culverts that are handling run-off from higher ground.

Cut and fill lots generally provide the greatest drainage problems, and the risk of failure is highest when the land has been seriously disturbed. By destroying the natural drainage patterns, the cut-and-fill builder imposes new weight build-ups that can tax the old grade unless carefully engineered. In cut-and-fill tracts, drainage systems are set up over a wide area with both underground catch basins and surface drains. These systems are intricate, however, and the individual homeowner must be careful with any auxiliary system he might want to design or even with any extensive landscaping that will change the contours of the lot. Some sale contracts specify that the builder will not be responsible if the buyer alters the drainage, so you should always contact the builder and his soils engineer before making any drastic cuts or placing new fill over the old.

Septic tanks

Of all the problems that may face the buyer of a hillside lot, inadequate drainage for a septic tank is the only one that can't be solved by better engineering and more money.

If you plan to build in an outlying area where there is no sewer system, you must submit a percolation report for the proposed septic tank before the building permit will be issued. Some cities require only proof of adequate percolation; others may want to see plans for the entire plumbing system. If conditions are unsatisfactory, then you must wait until a sewer system is installed before you go ahead with construction.

Rock and expansive soil hillsides are the most troublesome. You may be able

Roof, sidewall and floor fire: protecting a hillside house...

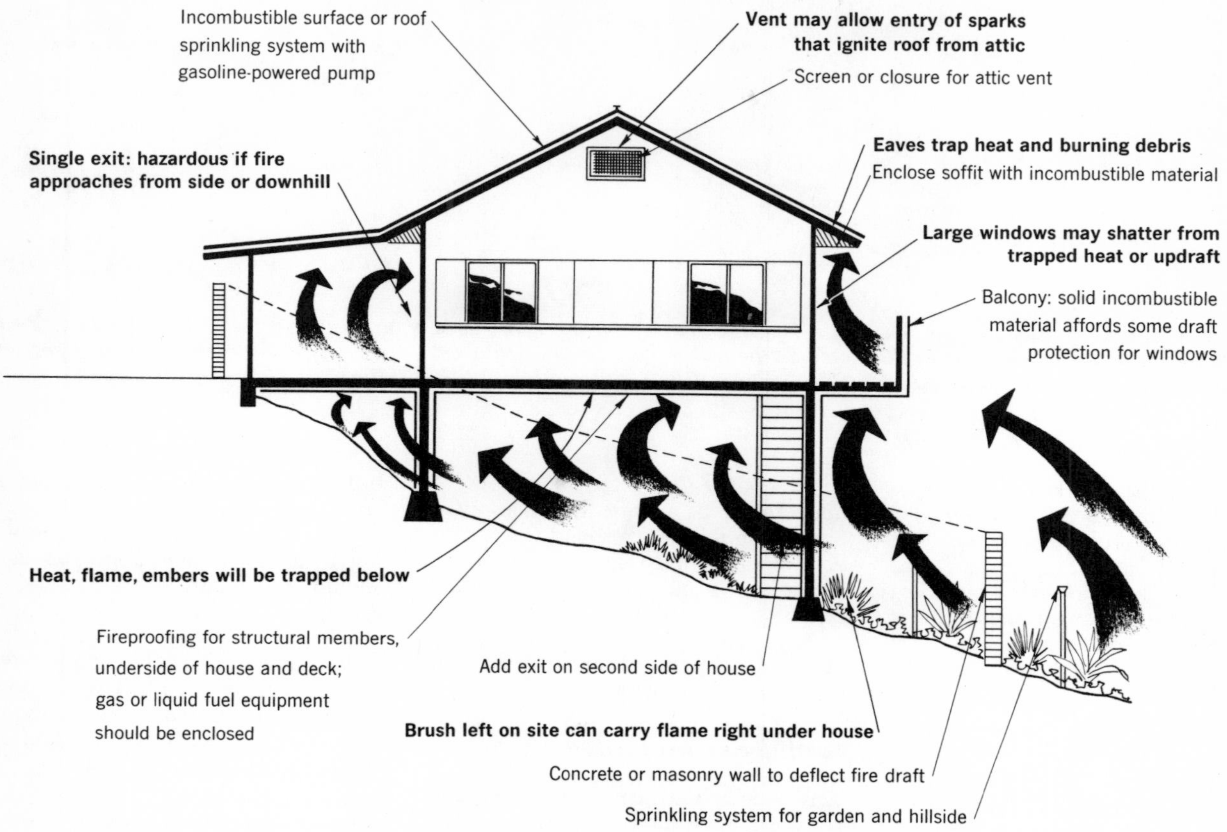

Incombustible surface or roof sprinkling system with gasoline-powered pump

Vent may allow entry of sparks that ignite roof from attic

Screen or closure for attic vent

Single exit: hazardous if fire approaches from side or downhill

Eaves trap heat and burning debris

Enclose soffit with incombustible material

Large windows may shatter from trapped heat or updraft

Balcony: solid incombustible material affords some draft protection for windows

Heat, flame, embers will be trapped below

Fireproofing for structural members, underside of house and deck; gas or liquid fuel equipment should be enclosed

Add exit on second side of house

Brush left on site can carry flame right under house

Concrete or masonry wall to deflect fire draft

Sprinkling system for garden and hillside

Some hazards *to a hillside house are shown in bold type. Some protective measures you can take are shown in light type.*

to dig below the bothersome strata to find an acceptable layer of porous material, but these cases are rare.

If you are to have a septic tank, check into the potential percolation field *before* you grade any part of the lot. In some cases, grading can destroy the only acceptable percolation field.

In a few isolated instances, you may encounter a well-developed hillside on which many septic tanks have been installed, but where you will not be allowed to put in another. The hill may have the maximum number of septic fields that it can handle, even though there are still open lots. In this case, you will have to delay construction until a sewer system is installed.

Fire protection

Hillside homes often have extra fire protection problems. The terrain generally does more to encourage the spread of fire than does flat land. The design of the house often includes open areas underneath that are susceptible to flames. Many sites have very limited access and turn-around room, so firefighting equipment cannot function smoothly. And much of the charm associated with hillside homes comes from the native growth that crowds around the buildings to provide a natural setting and natural fuel for a fire.

There is no way to completely fireproof a house, but there are several aspects of fire prevention that should be explored by prospective hillside dwellers.

• Location. Exposure to wind and the presence of uncleared slopes near the property increase fire danger.

• Access. Houses on narrow, winding streets and on cul-de-sacs with no turn-around room at the end do not give firefighters a chance. Some city codes specify street widths; 20 feet is a good general rule if there is no specific stipulation.

• Brush. The most important step you can take to protect your home is to isolate it as much as possible from native grass and chaparral that feed fire. Any home owner living in a potentially

Basic principles of earthquake-resistant construction

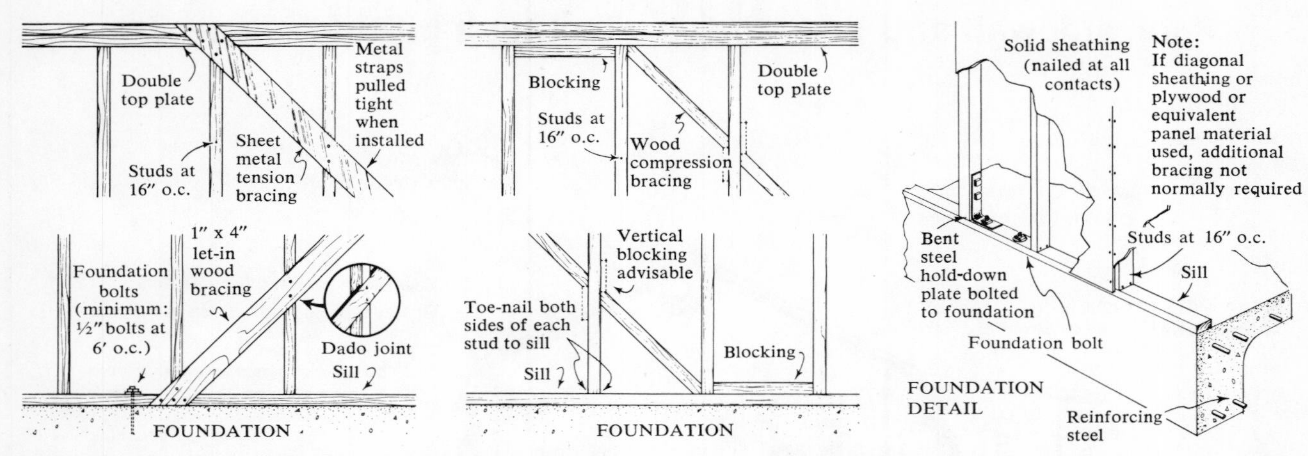

To increase *earthquake resistance in new house construction, sill should be bolted to foundation and all the studs toe-nailed to the sill. Cross-wall bracing should be installed in opposing pairs, either as* **X** *or* **V**. *Sketch at right shows how extra resistance is obtained by use of plywood sheathing and specially-designed hold down plates.*

hazardous area should keep clearing his own fire-resistant break between the house and the brush and grass. This break doesn't necessarily have to be skinned to the bare ground: Lawn, ivy, and other low-growing ground covers are fire-resistant. The break between brush or grass and the house should be a minimum of 30 feet in width, although a wider break is advisable.

- Water supply. In a major fire, pressure undoubtedly will drop in city mains. One safeguard is an auxiliary system, or you can place a pond or pool within 20 feet of unhindered access for a fire pumper.
- Materials and structure. A second line of defense (after brush clearance) is summed up in the drawing on this page. These precautions increase a house's chance of surviving a fire of moderate intensity. Some city and county codes now specify that any opening under the house that is eight feet or less in height must be enclosed with continuous walls.

Rates for fire insurance are established for a given area according to the over-all quality of its fire protection system. Many of the items considered are beyond the control of the individual homeowner. If you live in a brush-fire area, however, you can qualify for rate reductions on two counts:

- Roof composition. A reduction is allowed if the roof is of some more fire-retardant material than wood.
- Brush clearance. Reductions go into effect when brush is cleared at least 30 feet from the house, and increase with greater distances.

To qualify for these reductions, a house must be within five miles of a fire station that will respond (this situation applies in most incorporated brush fire areas). It must also be within 1,000 feet of a fire hydrant. And the house must be accessible to fire-fighting equipment, on an improved road wide enough for fire trucks to maneuver.

Earthquake protection

Any hillside home can be engineered to resist extensive earthquake damage. But it must be on good, solid soil, and be designed to accept great lateral forces. Earthquakes cause their greatest damage when they impose this lateral stress on structural designs that are primarily concerned with vertical stress.

There are two critical points that apply to hillside houses in particular:

- The foundation. The intensity of earthquake shock is directly related to the type of soil supporting the building. Structures built on solid rock stand the best chance of survival, while those on fill or loose natural ground are the most susceptible. Fill for cut-and-fill lots must be engineered for maximum strength; if it is not properly compacted, there may be differential settling during or after the earthquake that can break the back of a house.
- Lateral bracing. The house must be well-braced and be structurally continuous so it will move as a unit. Secure anchoring and proper bonds between foundation, frame, outer and inner walls, all floors and the roof will give the house the best chance.

If your community has a building code that conforms with the earthquake provisions of the uniform building code, then your approved design should be relatively safe from the standpoint of injury to occupants, and should be able to stand up under a serious quake with only minimum damage. Often, an architect or structural engineer can increase the earthquake resistance of your house without substantially increasing the cost.

Roads and driveways

If you decide on a lot in a remote area, be sure you know the status of the road that leads to your new residence. Most important is whether it is maintained by some public agency and has not been legally abandoned. If the road is not a city or county road, then you may be obligated to maintain it yourself or face the problems of forming an assessment district to rebuild it according to specified standards so the city or county will again assume its maintenance.

Once you find out who maintains the street, inquire about future improvements in grades, sidewalks and drainage. If you know that the street will be altered in the near future, you can plan ahead so your driveway will come out at the right level and still be on an acceptable incline. If you go ahead with construction without making such allowances, you may lose some of your cherished parking space, or worse yet, be faced with an extensive remodeling job to make your garage and driveway conform with standards of the new roadway.

Index

Photo Credits

American Plywood Assoc.: 119 (next to bottom), 123 (bottom). Barry Anderson: 61 (bottom), 65 (bottom). William Aplin: 61 (top, next to top), 63 (top left, top right, center right), 71 (next to top), 74 (bottom), 76, 77, 78 (center), 86 (center right), 98 (top right), 102 (bottom), 104 (top), 108 (bottom), 109 (bottom), 111 (top, bottom center), 112 (top left). Aplin-Dudley Studios: 63 (bottom left), 70 (bottom center), 86 (center left), 97 (top right), 98 (top left), 111 (bottom right), 112 (top right), 117 (top right). Morley Baer: 7 (top), 14, 15, 63 (bottom right), 66 (bottom left), 71 (top), 82, 83, 90 (top), 91 (top right), 97 (top left), 98 (bottom right). Miles Berne: 68 (bottom right). Jerry Bragstad: 100 (bottom right). Mimi Brandes: 115 (bottom right). Ernest Braun: 28, 29, 37 (bottom), 38, 39, 47 (next to top), 52, 53, 54, 55, 62 (left, bottom right), 68 (top left), 85 (top left), 86 (top right), 90 (center, bottom), 97 (bottom center), 102 (center), 103 (center right, bottom right), 106 (right), 107 (bottom right), 115 (top, bottom left). Tom Burns, Jr.: 12, 13, 19 (top), 22, 23, 47 (top), 56, 57, 70 (bottom left), 105 (center). Camera Hawaii: 70 (top left). Clyde Childress: 62 (top right). Glenn M. Christiansen: 19 (next to bottom), 26, 27, 104 (bottom center). Columbia Studios: 86 (bottom). Kenneth Cooperrider: 4 (right). Lyn Davis: 86 (top left), 91 (bottom left). Richard Dawson: 97 (bottom left). Dearborn-Massar: 7 (next to top), 10, 11, 19 (next to top), 20, 21, 24, 25, 30, 31, 37 (top), 40, 41, 47 (next to bottom), 48, 49, 61 (next to bottom), 66 (bottom right), 98 (bottom left), 109 (next to top), 111 (bottom left). Max Eckert: 71 (bottom), 102 (top), 103 (top left), 108 (top right). Philip Fein: 64 (bottom left). Richard Fish: 69 (top right, bottom), 78 (bottom left), 79 (bottom), 89, 92 (top, bottom), 101 (bottom left). Joern Gerdts: 37 (next to top, next to bottom), 42, 43. Bert Goldrath: 113. John Hartley: 75 (top right). Walter Houk: 101 (bottom right). Art Hupy: 74 (top). George Knight: 71 (next to bottom), 84 (top left). Elsa Knoll: 84 (bottom), 112 (bottom). Samson B. Knoll: 78 (bottom right). Roy Krell: 70 (bottom right), 79 (top left), 88 (bottom), 96, 100 (top left, bottom left), 105 (bottom left), 109 (top, next to bottom), 114 (bottom right), 116, 117 (top left), 118. Edmund Y. Lee: 70 (top right). Martin Photo: 70 (top center). E. W. Marugg: 107 (top, bottom left). Ken Molino: 103 (top right). Joe Munroe: 65 (top), 75 (top left). Don Normark: 68 (top right), 78 (top right), 105 (bottom right). Theodore Osmundson: 105 (top left). Kurt E. Oswald: 84 (top right). Phil Palmer: 91 (bottom right). Maynard L. Parker: 50, 51. Charles R. Pearson: 64 (bottom right), 67 (left), 86 (center). Photo-Craft Co.—Hawaii: 75 (bottom left). Gerald Ratto: 44, 45. Karl H. Riek: 103 (center left, bottom left). Tom Riley: 69 (top center). Katherine L. Robertson: 85 (bottom center). Martha Rosman: 69 (top left). Charles Schneider: 104 (bottom left). Julius Shulman: 34, 35, 67 (right), 108 (top left). Douglas M. Simmonds: 68 (bottom left). Shan Stewart: 79 (top right). Hugh N. Stratford: 7 (next to bottom), 16, 17, 19 (bottom), 32, 33. Roger Sturtevant: 7 (bottom), 8, 9, 47 (bottom), 58, 59, 88 (top). The British Travel Assoc.: 5 (right). Darrow Watt: 64 (top), 100 (top right), 101 (top), 110, 119 (next to top), 123 (top). R. Wenkam: 4 (left), 66 (top), 75 (bottom right), 78 (top left), 85 (top right), 85 (bottom right), 106 (left), 119 (top, bottom), 124. Mason Weymouth: 105 (top right). S. C. Wilson: 80, 81.